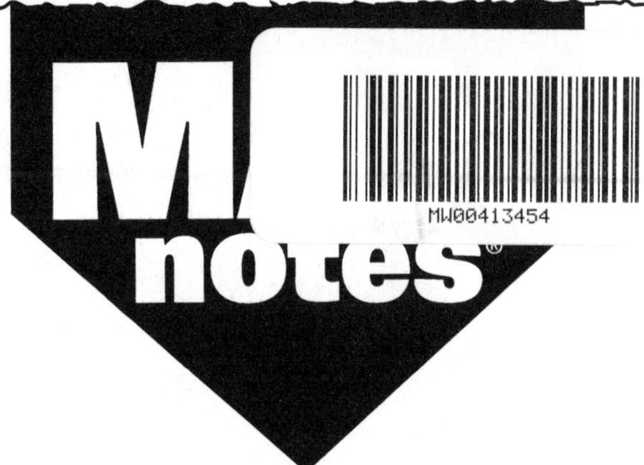

Jonathan Swift's

Gulliver's Travels

Text by
Stephen A. Stertz
(Ph.D., The University of Michigan)
Adjunct Assistant Professor of History
Kean College
Union, New Jersey

Illustrations by
Scott Nickerson

Research & Education Association

MAXnotes® for
GULLIVER'S TRAVELS

Printed in the United States of America

Library of Congress Catalog Card Number 96-67403

International Standard Book Number 0-87891-015-8

What **MAXnotes®** *Will Do for You*

This book is intended to help you absorb the essential contents and features of Jonathan Swift's *Gulliver's Travels* and to help you gain a thorough understanding of the work. The book has been designed to do this more quickly and effectively than any other study guide.

For best results, this **MAXnotes** book should be used as a companion to the actual work, not instead of it. The interaction between the two will greatly benefit you.

To help you in your studies, this book presents the most up-to-date interpretations of every section of the actual work, followed by questions and fully explained answers that will enable you to analyze the material critically. The questions also will help you to test your understanding of the work and will prepare you for discussions and exams.

Meaningful illustrations are included to further enhance your understanding and enjoyment of the literary work. The illustrations are designed to place you into the mood and spirit of the work's settings.

The **MAXnotes** also include summaries, character lists, explanations of plot, and section-by-section analyses. A biography of the author and discussion of the work's historical context will help you put this literary piece into the proper perspective of what is taking place.

The use of this study guide will save you the hours of preparation time that would ordinarily be required to arrive at a complete grasp of this work of literature. You will be well prepared for classroom discussions, homework, and exams. The guidelines that are included for writing papers and reports on various topics will prepare you for any added work which may be assigned.

The **MAXnotes** will take your grades "to the max."

Dr. Max Fogiel
Program Director

Contents

Each Chapter includes List of Characters, Summary, Analysis, Study Questions and Answers, and Suggested Essay Topics.

SECTION ONE

Introduction

The Life and Times of Jonathan Swift

Jonathan Swift, dean of St. Patrick's Cathedral in Dublin, was a major figure in literature and politics in both Ireland and England. He was famous in his own time as a witty satirist of many aspects of life. He later became world-famous as the author of a children's classic, *Gulliver's Travels,* which was not originally intended by its author as a children's book. He was born in Dublin to a well-to-do family partly of English descent, was educated at Trinity College, Dublin, and Oxford University, and worked as secretary to the retired politician Sir William Temple. These other experiences acquainted him with the vanity and follies of leading figures in British life. Later, after difficulties in obtaining employment as a clergyman of the Church of England, he increased his acquaintance with fashionable society and acquired the tinge of bitterness that characterizes much of his literary work.

At the beginning of the eighteenth century, Swift (already a fashionable satirist), received the degree of Doctor of Divinity from the University of Dublin and began to write political satires. In 1704, having already published some widely-read political works, Swift became famous with the publication of *The Battle of the Books* and *The Tale of a Tub.* Other satirical works spread Swift's fame to London, which he visited frequently. Swift was a major figure in the Tory party as well as a journalist and writer when, in 1713, he became the dean of St. Patrick's Cathedral, the Anglican (Episcopal) cathedral of Dublin. As dean, he was assistant to the bishop, supervising the cathedral's day-to-day affairs.

Although he never married, Swift had a long and close friendship with Esther Johnson, known to him as Stella, to whom the published diary called the *Journal to Stella* was addressed. After becoming dean, Swift met Ester Vanhomrigh, daughter of a wealthy merchant. He called her "Vanessa," and they too had a close friendship. In 1723, Vanessa, hearing of Swift's friendship with Stella, died.

Gulliver's Travels, which Swift began writing by 1720, was published anonymously in 1726. Additional successful satirical works were written in the following years, but as Swift grew old, his health deteriorated. In 1742, after suffering several strokes, he was declared insane. He died several years later in 1745.

Swift's numerous works, including articles as well as books, attacked many of the evils of his time, particularly political corruption and the oppression of the Irish by the English. His wit and satire attract, amuse, and educate the reader.

Historical Background

The age in which Swift lived is sometimes called the Augustan Age. British writers and artists of the time admired the order and sophistication of the culture of classical Rome during the reign of the Emperor Augustus, about 1,700 years earlier. Satire in Swift's time was modeled on works translated into English satirizing the weaknesses of society and politics in Roman times. These authors, as well as later satirists, influenced Swift.

Although England first invaded Ireland in the early Middle Ages, it was only during the reign of Elizabeth, about a hundred years before Swift's birth, that English control became complete. Most of the Irish had remained Roman Catholics after the English went over to Anglican Protestantism in the sixteenth century. Swift's family was Anglican, and they were part of the elite living in Dublin that was known as "the Ascendancy", because it included the most powerful people in Ireland.

During the English Civil War, radical English Protestants had oppressed the Irish Catholic, depriving them of property and civil rights. After the restoration of the English monarchy in 1660, six years before Swift's birth, much of this oppression continued, although King James II, a Catholic, gave religious freedom to Catholics. After his overthrow in 1689, King William and Queen Mary became sovereigns of Britain and Ireland. Britain became a limited monarchy under the control of the British Parliament, and Catholics were again deprived of many of their rights. In England, religious freedom for Protestants who were not Anglicans was limited. Swift protested against many of these limitations of freedom and against commercial restrictions on Ireland.

Under the limited monarchy, two political parties began to compete in elections for Parliament—the Whigs, who represented merchants and non-Anglican Protestants called "Dissenters;" and the Tories, who wanted to strengthen Parliament who represented wealthy landowners, and also wanted to strengthen the Anglican Church and make the king more powerful. Swift, an Anglican dean, was a Tory.

Britain was modernizing. The Bank of England was established, trading in stocks and bonds became important, the cities grew, international commerce increased, and the Royal Society was established to conduct scientific research. Swift satirized many of these tendencies in *Gulliver's Travels* and elsewhere.

In literature, early forms of the novel, often involving travel and adventure, were being written. Poetry and plays were often inspired by ancient Greek and Roman literature; they were carefully written and involved strict rules. Novels were often the more fanciful form of literature.

Master List of Characters

Lemuel Gulliver—*(a.k.a. The Man-Mountain, The Mannikin) Narrator of the Novel; a physician, ship's officer, and traveler.*

Mary Burton—*The patient wife of Lemuel Gulliver, a daughter of a London merchant who remains behind in England during his voyages.*

The Hurgo—*A high official of the Island of Lilliput, who feeds Gulliver after his capture and sends him to their Emperor.*

Richard Sympson—*Cousin of Lemuel Gulliver. The "Letter from Capt. Gulliver is addressed to him; Gulliver complains that his cousin has made alterations to the manuscript; "The Publisher to the Reader" is supposed to be written by Sympson.*

James Bates—*Surgeon who supports Gulliver's career.*

The Emperor of Lilliput—*The proud, sometimes tyrannical, ruler of the island kingdom.*

Flimnap—*Treasurer of Lilliput, who owes his office to his acrobatic ability.*

Reldresal—*Principal Secretary of Private Affairs of Lilliput, who befriends and tries to help Gulliver.*

Skyresh Bolgolam—*High Admiral of Lilliput and member of the governing council, he is the chief enemy Gulliver faces in Lilliput.*

The Treasurer's Wife—*Wife of Flimnap, who frequently visits Gulliver, accompanied by a retinue; Gulliver vindicates her honor by proving that they were never alone.*

The Empress—*Another enemy of Gulliver, who favors his punishment because he put out a fire in the palace in an inappropriate way.*

"A Considerable person at court"—*Visits Gulliver and privately gives him a copy of the articles of impeachment against him.*

The Emperor of Blefuscu—*Ruler of Lilliput's rival kingdom, who protects Gulliver after he escapes there, having been accused of treason by the Lilliputians.*

The Farmer's Servant—*The giant Brobdingnagian picks up Gulliver and takes him to his master.*

The Farmer—*The Brobdingnagian who exhibits Gulliver as a curiosity.*

The Farmer's Wife—*At first disgusted by Gulliver as though he were a spider, she is sympathetic later.*

Glumdalclitch—*"Little nurse" in Brobdingnagian; the farmer's daughter makes Gulliver her pet, and continues to take care of him after he is bought by the Queen of Brobdingnag.*

The Queen of Brobdingnag—*Buys Gulliver from the farmer and presents him to the King.*

The King—*Ruler of Brobdingnag, a patron of scholarship; asks Gulliver to describe England to him.*

The Queen's Dwarf—*Becomes Gulliver's enemy because his place as the smallest person at court has been usurped.*

The Maids of Honor—*They play with Gulliver and undress in his presence, which he finds disgusting because of their immense size.*

The Officers—*Officials who search Gulliver and make an inventory of his belongings.*

Thomas Wilcocks—*English sea captain who rescues Gulliver and takes him back to England after the box in which he was carried in Brobdingnag falls into the sea; thinks Gulliver is crazy.*

Captain William Robinson—*Invites Gulliver on his third voyage.*

Clustril and Drunlo—*The Treasurer's informers.*

The Dutchman—*One of the pirates who attack Gulliver's ship.*

The Japanese Pirate—*Sets Gulliver adrift after his ship is captured.*

The King of the Flying Island of Laputa—*Interested only in mathematics, science, and astronomy; asks Gulliver only about these subjects.*

The Court Official—*Related to the King of Laputa; intervenes with him to allow Gulliver to leave the Flying Island for Balnibarbi, the continent on the ground beneath it.*

The Lord Munodi—*Official, former governor of Lagado; describes the continent to Gulliver; shows him the Academy.*

First Scholar—*Member of the Academy of Lagado; tries to extract sunbeams from cucumbers.*

Second Scholar—*Tries to reduce human excrement to its original food.*

Architect—*Tries to build houses from the top down.*

Blind Artist—*Leads apprentices, also blind, mixing paint colors by smell.*

Projector—*Tries to plow the ground with hogs.*

Artist—*Tries to use spiders as silkworms.*

Physician—*Tries to cure people by pumping them with a bellow.*

Universal Artist—*Tries a variety of impossible experiments.*

Speculative Professor—*Makes a frame with all words in the Lagadan language written on pieces of wood; composes nonsensical literary works by rearranging them at random.*

Language Professors—*They try to substitute images of things discussed for words, eliminating the necessity of speaking.*

Mathematical Professor—*Tries to teach by giving students pills containing knowledge.*

Political Professor—*Tries to cure politicians with medicine and violence.*

Second and Third Political Professors—*Propose absurd methods of taxation.*

Fourth Political Professor—*Tries to discover conspiracies against the government by studying people's food.*

Governor of Glubbdubdrib—*Has ghosts for servants; acts as host to Gulliver; calls up spirits of famous historical figures at Gulliver's request.*

Custom-House Officer—*Confines Gulliver in Luggnagg.*

King of Luggnagg—*Acts as Gulliver's host; Gulliver is invited to stay permanently, but he refuses.*

Struldbruggs—*Immortal Luggnaggians who lack eternal youth and are therefore unable to do much or remember anything.*

Emperor of Japan—*Suspects Gulliver of being a Christian after he refuses to trample on a crucifix.*

James Welch—*Mutineer on the* Adventure, *who sets Gulliver adrift.*

The Dapple-Grey—*Houyhnhm (rational horse) who protects Gulliver and asks him about his country.*

The Sorrel Nag—*Servant of the Dapple-Gray.*

Member of Assembly of Houyhnhms—*Proposes to eliminate the Yahoos.*

The Yahoos—*Animal-like savage human beings in the country of the Houyhnhms.*

Captain Pedro de Mendez—*Takes Gulliver to Portugal after he is expelled from the land of the Houyhnhms.*

Summary of the Novel

In *Gulliver's Travels*, Gulliver describes his four voyages. In the first voyage, he is the only person to reach land after a shipwreck. He awakes to find himself tied down by tiny men; these are the Lilliputians. A *Hurgo* (official) supervises them. Gulliver agrees to cooperate, and is untied and taken to the capital where he meets Lilliput's Emperor. He agrees to serve the Lilliputians, and is granted partial freedom in return. Gulliver prevents an invasion from Lilliput's enemy, Blefuscu, by stealing the enemy's ships and is given a high title of honor. He makes friends and enemies at court and learns details of Lilliputian society. After putting out a fire in the palace by urinating on it, he is accused of high treason through polluting the palace. He is sentenced to be blinded and starved. However, Gulliver escapes to Blefuscu, finds a boat, sails out to sea, and is picked up by an English ship.

Two months after his return to England, Gulliver leaves on his second voyage. He lands in an unknown country to get water and is abandoned. A giant reaper picks him up (he is in the country of the gigantic Brobdingnagians) and takes him to a farmer, who wants him to be on exhibit as a freak. He fights a gigantic cat and other monstrous animals. The Queen of Brobdingnag buys Gulliver and presents him to the King. The farmer's daughter, Glumdalclitch, who had befriended Gulliver, is hired by the King as Gulliver's guardian and nurse. Gulliver quarrels with the King's dwarf, but describes England in detail to the King. Gulliver is carried around in a box and tours the kingdom. He fights birds and animals and finds the King's Maids of Honor, who undress before him, disgusting him because of their great size. Gulliver's box is picked up by a gigantic eagle and dropped into the sea; he is picked up by an English ship and returns to England.

Shortly after his return, Gulliver leaves on his third voyage. His ship is captured by pirates, who set him adrift in a small boat. He arrives on the flying island of Laputa, which flies over the continent of Balnibarbi. The people he meets are interested only in abstract speculations. Their king asks Gulliver only about mathematics in England. Gulliver learns that the island is kept flying by magnetism. He travels to Balnibarbi, and he is shown the

Academy of Laputa, where scholars devote all their time to absurd inventions and ideas. He then goes to Glubbdubdrib, an island of magicians. The king is waited on by ghosts, and he calls up the ghosts of dead historical characters at Gulliver's request. He then goes to Luggnagg, where the Struldbruggs who have eternal life but not eternal youth. After spending time in Japan, Gulliver returns to England.

On his fourth voyage, Gulliver is set on shore in an unknown land by mutineers. This is the land of the Houyhnhms: intelligent, rational horses who hold as servants repulsive animal-like human beings called Yahoos. A dapple-gray Houyhnhm who becomes his master is unable to understand the frailties and emotions in Gulliver's account of England. The Assembly is distressed at the idea of a partly-rational Yahoo living with a Houyhnhm, votes to expel Gulliver. He makes a boat and is picked up by a Portuguese ship. On his return to England, Gulliver is so disgusted with human beings that he refuses to associate with them, preferring the company of horses.

Estimated Reading Time

Three weeks should be allowed for the study of *Gulliver's Travels.* Two weeks will be required to read the novel, reading four chapters at a sitting. The student should read every day from Monday to Friday. After reading the chapters, the student should answer all study questions in this guide to ensure understanding and comprehension. The essay questions may be used if needed. The fourth week is set aside for reports, projects, and testing as deemed necessary by the teacher.

SECTION TWO

Part I: A Voyage to Lilliput

"Letter from Capt. Gulliver to his Cousin Sympson", "The Publisher to the Reader", and Chapters 1, 2, 3, and 4

New Characters:

Lemuel Gulliver: *an English physician, ship's officer, and traveler who is the narrator of the novel*

Richard Sympson: *cousin of the narrator; the "Letter from Capt. Gulliver" is addressed to him; Gulliver complains that his cousin has made alterations in his manuscript; "The Publisher to the Reader" is supposed to be written by Sympson, who says that the work has an air of truth*

James Bates: *surgeon who supports Gulliver's career*

Mary Burton: *Gulliver's wife, daughter of a London merchant*

The Hurgo: *Lilliputian official who supervises Gulliver's capture, feeds him, and sends him to the Emperor*

The Emperor of Lilliput: *the proud and sometimes tyrannical ruler of the island kingdom*

The Officers: *officials who search Gulliver and make an inventory of his belongings*

Flimnap: *Treasurer of Lilliput, who owes his office to his athletic ability, a typically flexible and adaptable politician*

Reldresal: *Principal Secretary of Private Affairs of Lilliput, who befriends and tries to help Gulliver*

Skyresh Bolgolam: *High Admiral of Lilliput and member of the governing council, chief enemy of Gulliver in Lilliput; has a morose and sour complexion*

Summary

In the "Letter from Capt. Gulliver to his Cousin Sympson," Gulliver complains that his cousin, Richard Sympson, the publisher of his book, has made alterations without the author's consent. He complains that the publication proved useless, because the description of an ideal society in the book did not end the imperfections of human society in seven months. He denies that the book is a fiction. In "The Publisher to the Reader", Richard Sympson states that the book has an air of truth and that he has left out only certain technical points of interest only to sailors.

In Chapter One, Gulliver describes his family background and medical education. After his apprenticeship to the surgeon James Bates, Gulliver studied both surgery and navigation, going on a voyage as a ship's doctor. He returns to England, marries Mary Burton, daughter of a London merchant, practices in London, makes several voyages, and finally goes on a voyage to the Pacific, where a storm sinks the ship. Gulliver alone reaches the shore of an island. He falls asleep, finds himself tied down by men six inches tall, is attacked by arrows, and is finally partly untied by an official, the *Hurgo,* who feeds him and sends him to the Emperor of Lilliput.

Gulliver cooperates with and amuses the Emperor and the Lilliputians in the hope of soon getting his freedom back. He begins to learn their language and sees a show in which people hoping for political advancement perform difficult and dangerous acrobatic feats. At times, the Emperor demands that high officials perform such feats to show that they have kept their ability. Flimnap, the high treasurer, and Reldresal, principal secretary for private affairs, are the best acrobats in the kingdom. Awards are also offered for the best leaping and creeping. Gulliver holds up

soldiers performing military exercises and even the Empress herself. Gulliver's hat is restored to him; he stands like a colossus over troops who pass under him.

Finally, the cabinet and the full council approve Gulliver's petition for liberty, with only Skyresh Bolgolam, the High Admiral, opposed. Bolgolam finally approves Gulliver's liberation—provided that the conditions are drawn up by him. Swift then gives the full text of the agreement. Gulliver must not leave Lilliput without the Emperor's permission, must stay out of the capital without his order, must confine his walks to the main roads, must be careful not to step on anyone or anything, must carry messages monthly (complete with messenger and horse), must be the ally of Lilliput against its traditional enemy, Blefuscu, and must perform various other services appropriate to his size. In return he has a daily food allowance and free access to the Emperor. His chains are then unlocked in the Emperor's presence.

Gulliver tours the capital, Mildendo, with the Emperor's permission. The city is described; Gulliver examines the imperial palace using two stools made of trees. He temporarily removes the roof to see inside. Reldresal, principal secretary of private affairs, visits Gulliver and discusess Lilliput's problems with him. Lilliput is troubled internally by party strife between those who wear low heels on their shoes and those who wear high heels. Externally, it is threatened by the neighboring island of Blefuscu. The struggle between these islands originated in a dispute over which end of an egg should be broken before eating it.

Analysis

In the "Letter from Capt. Gulliver," Swift displays dramatic irony, showing Gulliver as a vain man who expects his description of the ideal society of the Houyhnhms to reform English society in seven months. Another example of dramatic irony is the statement that some critics are so bold as to think his travels a mere fiction. Dramatic irony is also found in "The Publisher to the Reader," where the publisher states that "there is an air of truth apparent through the whole." Swift is satirizing fantastic books of travel to exotic, newly discovered places, which were popular in his time, as well as works

of fiction such as *Robinson Crusoe* or the earlier but still popular description of an ideal society, Thomas More's *Utopia*.

In Chapter One of *Gulliver's Travels*, the narrator begins by giving a short, realistic statement of his life up to his first voyage, to establish believability. After the description of the storm, Swift moves from realism to fantasy; this is done carefully so that there is a natural transition. Fantastic events are described in plain language, making it easier for the reader to believe them. Lilliput is carefully imagined, resulting in the book's later popularity as a children's book.

Swift's vision of the miniature world of Lilliput is elaborated physically through his description of the elaborate contrivances by which Gulliver is able to see inside the palace. It is described politically through the agreement between Gulliver and the Lilliputians. This technique heightens the reader's belief and satirizes legal and political documents as presented in newspapers, histories, and travel books of Swift's time.

As the chapters progress, it becomes increasingly obvious that the England of Swift's time is being satirized. Politicians gain success and royal favor by practicing difficult and dangerous maneuvers, here satirized by being presented literally as acrobatic tricks. The clash between two cultures, and two sizes, is shown by the inventory of Gulliver's belongings, which also satirizes legal documents. Gulliver himself is a sort of politician. He gains his freedom and then rises in Lilliputian society by cooperating with the powers that be.

Flimnap is usually identified as Sir Robert Walpole, England's first Prime Minister, a Whig, who was in office when *Gulliver's Travels* was published. Other characters have been identified, in some cases with more controversy, with other contemporary English statesmen; the general element of political satire in *Gulliver's Travels* is more important than particular identifications.

In Chapter Four, Gulliver says that he is not giving a detailed description and history of Lilliput because he is reserving this information for "a greater work, which is now ready for the press." Here, he is both satirizing contemporary travel books and cleverly indicating that Lilliput is, apart from the size of its inhabitants, no

fantastic exotic country or Utopia. It is a country like England, as he has already hinted and will indicate when Reldresal tells Gulliver of his country's internal and external problems. The controversy within Lilliput between the high and low heels clearly represents trouble between the Tories and Whigs in England. This was a cause for alarm at the time, because political parties were a relative novelty, having first arisen in the 1680's.

The external conflict clearly satirizes relations between England and France, the latter represented by Blefuscu.

The conflict regarding the breaking of eggs represents the schism separating Protestants and Catholics. Swift, a clergyman of the Church of England in heavily Catholic Ireland, had already satirized theological differences in *A Tale of a Tub.* Swift has been interpreted here in two ways—that political and religious conflicts are as trivial as eggs and shoes, that people are trivializing important controversies. The satire is effective in both directions.

Gulliver has already agreed in writing to help Lilliput against Belfuscu, and the talk with Redresal strengthens his resolve. A less talented writer might have Gulliver say that he is reminded of his own country, but such a clumsy device would spoil or weaken the satire.

Study Questions

1. Where does Gulliver meet the Emperor?
2. How is Gulliver fed?
3. Why does the Lilliputian government go to such trouble to feed and shelter Gulliver if he is so dangerous because of his size?
4. What does the inventory of Gulliver's belongings tell the reader about the differences between Lilliput and England?
5. How does Gulliver ingratiate himself to the Emperor?
6. Why does Gulliver cooperate with the Lilliputians?
7. What are some of the shows Gulliver sees and participates in, and how do high government officials participate in them?

8. What is the purpose of the agreement between Gulliver and the Lilliputians?
9. Who is Gulliver's worst enemy at the Lilliputian court?
10. What are the main problems of Lilliput, as described to Gulliver by Reldresal?

Answers

1. Gulliver meets the Emperor for the first time in the house where he is being kept.
2. To feed Gulliver, the villages around the capital provide six beeves (oxen), forty sheep, and a proportionate quantity of other foods and beverages.
3. The Lilliputian government goes to great trouble to provide for Gulliver's needs because he can be used as an ally against the enemy country, Blefuscu.
4. The inventory of Gulliver's belongings tells the reader both about the difference of scale between the Lilliputians and the English and about their lack of familiarity with such things as tobacco, watches and gunpowder.
5. Gulliver ingratiates himself with the Emperor by agreeing to perform in various shows. The difference in size between himself and the Lilliputians is a source of entertainment.
6. Gulliver cooperates with the Lilliputians in order to convince them to unchain and free him.
7. The shows Gulliver sees and participates in include military and acrobatic exercises; high government officials participate in dangerous acrobatic stunts in order to show their dexterity.
8. The purpose of the agreement between Gulliver and the Lilliputians is to get Gulliver to help them both in domestic matters (carrying messages, helping in construction

projects, surveying the coastline) and in the war against Blefuscu. In exchange, he receives his freedom, subject to certain conditions.

9. Gulliver's worst enemy at the Lilliputian court is Skyresh Bolgolam, the Admiral of the Realm.
10. According to Reldresal in his conversation with Gulliver, the chief problems of Lilliput are the domestic quarrel, which has at times resulted in violence, between the high-heel and low-heel parties or factions, and the long war over the religious question of which end of an egg to break before eating it.

Suggested Essay Topics

1. Discuss Gulliver's progress from chained alien to important ally of the Lilliputians.
2. Define satire and describe how it is used in these chapters, using examples from the text.
3. Discuss the transitions in the tone of these chapters, from travel book to description of an alien society to satire on English politics.
4. Discuss the relationships between Gulliver and the Emperor of Lilliput, Skyresh Bolgolam, and Reldresal.

Chapters 5 and 6

New Characters:

The Empress of Lilliput: *an enemy of Gulliver, who favors his punishment because he put out a fire in the palace in an inappropriate way*

The Treasurer's Wife: *wife of Flimnap, who frequently visits Gulliver, but accompanied by a retinue; Gulliver vindicates her honor by proving that they were never alone*

Clustril and Drunlo: *the Treasurer's informers cannot prove that anyone except the Treasurer (on the Emperor's express orders)* *came to Gulliver incognito, but successfully damaged Gulliver's reputation with the Treasurer and the Emperor*

Summary

Gulliver wades and swims to the enemy island, Blefuscu, eight hundred yards at its nearest point from Lilliput, and prevents an invasion of Lilliput. He pulls away the fleet of Blefuscu by tying ropes to the ships and pulling the ropes, thus taking the ships to Lilliput. He shields himself from the enemy's arrows with his eyeglasses. As a result, Gulliver is created a *Nardac*, Lilliput's highest title of honor. The Emperor proposes that Gulliver do the same for all other ships of Blefuscu; Gulliver refuses, saying that as a result Blefuscu would be conquered by Lilliput. He would "never be an instrument of bringing a free and brave people into slavery." The cabinet of Lilliput agrees with Gulliver, but the Emperor and many high officials then become enemies of Gulliver and plot against him. Blefuscu asks for peace; Gulliver's contact with the ambassadors increases the dislike the Emperor and certain Lilliputian officials have for Gulliver.

When a fire breaks out in the imperial palace, Gulliver puts it out by urinating on it, violating a law and increasing the Empress's hatred of him.

In Chapter Six, Gulliver breaks the narrative temporarily and describes the institutions and customs of Lilliput. It appears to be a Utopian society with enlightened methods of childbearing; laws are strict; ingratitude is a crime and "disbelief of a Divine Providence" makes a man ineligible for public office. In recent years, however, Lilliputian society has decayed. In the last two generations, high officials had to show acrobatic proficiency, and things are now getting worse.

Gulliver then describes how furniture, linen, and clothing were made for him. He also describes his meals.

Toward the end of Chapter Six, the narrative resumes. The Emperor, various members of the royal family, and Flimnap the High Treasurer all dine with Gulliver. Flimnap, always Gulliver's secret enemy, tells the Emperor that because the cost of supporting Gulliver has damaged Lilliput's economy, Gulliver ought to be

discharged. Flimnap's wife, together with several other people, frequently visits Gulliver. Flimnap's informers, Clustril and Drunlo, make false charges against Gulliver, causing his influence with the Emperor to decline still more, although Gulliver is able to prove that he was never alone with the Treasurer's wife.

Analysis

Gulliver, like a great and successful general, is at the peak of his popularity after defeating Blefuscu. He can only decline in influence. In a satire of politics, this happens to him. He refuses to support the Emperor's ambition to conquer Blefuscu and there are court conspiracies against him. The incident of the fire makes things worse. The fall of statesmen in England in Swift's time is satirized. Swift then shows his ability to write in different narrative styles by describing Lilliput in the style of a writer describing an ideal society, such as Thomas More depicting *Utopia*. The contrast between this idealized description and the sleazy court intrigues in which Gulliver is involved is an example of Swift's use of dramatic irony. The naive Gulliver is intelligent enough to see the difference between the ideal and the reality, but ascribes it to fairly recent change in Lilliputian society. When the narrative resumes, Lilliput is seen as in fact a treacherous and ungrateful society, despite ingratitude being a serious crime on paper. Swift is here displaying a somewhat cynical view of human society in general, a view which is shown with greater intensity elsewhere in *Gulliver's Travels*. Gulliver's contact with the ambassadors of Blefuscu, however, provides an opportunity for a future escape from the trouble he is getting into in Lilliput. His great size and the ease of getting to the other island have already been demonstrated to the reader.

Study Questions

1. What is the great service performed by Gulliver to the Emperor of Lilliput, and what is his reward?
2. Does Gulliver's influence continue to increase?
3. What is the first event that gets Gulliver into trouble?
4. How does putting out the fire in the palace get Gulliver into deeper trouble?

5. How does Gulliver interrupt the narrative in Chapter Six?
6. How does Gulliver explain the difference between the ideal laws of Lilliput and its present corrupt condition?
7. How are children brought up in Lilliput?
8. What was Gulliver's daily life like in Lilliput?
9. What was the specific reason Flimnap gave in his conference with the Emperor for discharging Gulliver?
10. How did Gulliver "vindicate a great lady?"

Answers

1. Gulliver removes the fleet of Blefuscu by wading and swimming there and taking the ships to Lilliput with ropes, preventing an invasion of Lilliput. He is rewarded by being made a *Nardac*, Lilliput's highest title of honor.
2. Gulliver's influence declines, despite his services, because of intrigues.
3. The first event that gets Gulliver into trouble is his refusal to cooperate in the total conquest of Blefuscu, which antagonizes the Emperor.
4. Gulliver gets into deeper trouble because he has polluted the palace by putting out the fire by urinating on it.
5. Gulliver interrupts the narrative in Chapter Six by describing the laws and customs of Lilliput.
6. According to Gulliver, conditions began to decline in Lilliput during the reign of the grandfather of the current Emperor, when officials were first required to perform acrobatic feats. Things have gotten even worse in recent years.
7. In Lilliput, according to Gulliver, children are brought up in public nurseries and schools, not by the parents. They are brought up carefully, according to their sex and social condition.
8. Gulliver's daily life in Lilliput included making furniture for himself out of large trees, and being clothed and fed on a large scale by the Lilliputians.

9. Flimnap advised the Emperor to discharge Gulliver because the expense of supporting him was a strain on Lilliput's economy.
10. Gulliver vindicated Flimnap's wife by declaring that when she visited him she was accompanied by several other people.

Suggested Essay Topics

1. Discuss the decline of Gulliver's fortunes in Lilliput in Chapters Five and Six.
2. Define irony, and how it is used in Chapters Five and Six.
3. Discuss Swift's facility of changing from one narrative style to another, and discuss how these changes fit into the plan of the book.
4. Discuss the changes in Gulliver's relationship with the people of Blefuscu.

Chapters 7 and 8

New Characters:

"A Considerable person at Court": *visits Gulliver and privately gives him a copy of the articles of impeachment against him*

The Emperor of Blefuscu: *ruler who protects Gulliver after Gulliver, having been accused of treason by the Lilliputians, escapes to Blefuscu*

Mrs. Gulliver: *the patient wife of the narrator, who remains behind in England during his voyages; introduced earlier as Mary Burton, her maiden name*

Summary

In Chapters Seven and Eight Gulliver, who "had been all my life," as he says, "a stranger to Courts," discovers their terrible effects. He is privately informed by "a considerable person at Court" of the Lilliputians' charges against him. He is informed by this person that envy of his achievement in capturing the enemy's fleet has earned Gulliver the undying hatred of the admiral, Skyresh Bolgolam, and that Flimnap, the High Treasurer, has been antagonized by rumors about Gulliver and his lady. The articles of impeachment against Gulliver are shown to Gulliver and to the reader. The first article accuses Gulliver of ritual pollution by urinating on the imperial palace "under color of extinguishing the fire." The second article accuses him of treasonously refusing to seize all the ships of Blefuscu, protecting that island from conquest by Lilliput. The third article accuses him of inappropriate contact with the ambassadors from Blefuscu, while the fourth accuses him of planning to travel to Blefuscu with "only verbal license" (permission) from the Emperor of Lilliput.

Gulliver is informed by the court official that the Emperor had favored sparing Gulliver's life. Reldresal, because of his friendship with Gulliver, successfully pleaded to that effect, proposing that Gulliver be blinded, so he could still work for the Lilliputians. After the admiral and secretary demand a harsher punishment, the Emperor proposes that, in addition to being blinded, Gulliver should be gradually starved to death. This proposal is adopted.

The Emperor and court, in accordance with a recently-adopted practice, announce that this punishment is an example of the Emperor's "great leniency and tenderness." Gulliver decides to escape, and takes a ship with him (putting his clothes in it) to Blefuscu, where he is received by their Emperor with hospitality.

In Chapter Eight, Gulliver discovers a real boat in Blefuscu, and he has it repaired with some difficulty. After the Emperor of Blefuscu refuses to return him to Lilliput to be punished, Gulliver has sails put on the boat, loads it with food, and sets sail on the high seas. He is picked up by an English ship and returns to England, staying for only two months. Gulliver, being well provided for by an inheritance, leaves his wife and two children and goes on another voyage.

Analysis

In these chapters, we see Swift's bitterness against political intrigues, in part resulting from his personal experiences, expressed. Gulliver's cooperation and assistance to the Lilliputians merely excites their envy; he is almost sentenced to death, and the best that his friend Flimnap can do is get a sentence of blinding

and gradual starvation. The charges are an example of irony, since services and innocent acts are turned into acts of treason. Gulliver himself calls the punishment an "easy" one and says that his decision to escape is merely the result of "the precipitancy" (impulsiveness) "of youth." Swift is using the technique of dramatic irony; Gulliver is far more naive than Swift himself was. In fact, this is only the second time Gulliver acts uncooperatively toward the Lilliputians, the first being his refusal to destroy Blefuscu on their part. Swift is implicitly contrasting Gulliver's great size, compared to the Lilliputians, with his subordination to them and his near-agreement in his own blinding and starvation by men one-twelfth his size. Such cooperation might have been appropriate in ideal society, but Lilliput is in practice nothing of the sort, despite its idealized laws.

In Chapter Eight, Swift turns again to the difference of scale in describing Gulliver's fitting out of the boat. He returns again to the businesslike narrative at the beginning and end of a traveler's tale in describing Gulliver's return to England.

The element of political satire and the way Gulliver refuses to further participate in war, on either side, reflect Swift's support of the Tory element opposed to war with France. Although one-to-one identification of the characters with contemporary political figures is impossible, there is clearly an element of political allegory in *Gulliver's Travels.* Other elements are satire of human follies in general and of the traveler's tale and the idea of a perfect society in particular.

Study Questions

1. How does Gulliver hear of the charges against him?
2. What are the main charges brought against Gulliver by the Lilliputians?
3. What is the original proposed punishment of Gulliver, and what is the final punishment?
4. Who brings about the compromise regarding Gulliver's punishment?
5. How does Gulliver escape from the Lilliputians?
6. How does the Emperor of Blefuscu receive Gulliver?
7. How does Gulliver leave Blefuscu?
8. How does Gulliver get to England?
9. How long does he stay in England?
10. What enables him to go on his second voyage?

Answers

1. Gulliver is informed of the charges against him by "a considerable person at Court" who owed Gulliver a favor.

2. The main charges brought against Gulliver by the Lilliputians are polluting the palace by urinating on it, refusing to destroy Blefuscu by taking all its ships, having conversations with its ambassadors, and planning to go there.
3. The original proposed punishment of Gulliver is death; the final punishment, to which the Lilliputians sentence him, is blinding followed by gradual starvation.
4. The Principal Secretary for Private Affairs of Lilliput, Reldresal, Gulliver's friend, brings about the compromise by which Gulliver's life is to be spared.
5. Gulliver escapes from Lilliput by wading and swimming to Blefuscu, putting his clothes in a Lilliputian ship which he tows with him.
6. The Emperor of Blefuscu receives Gulliver with hospitality, refusing to send him back to Lilliput.
7. Gulliver finds a real boat on the island and has it fitted out, enabling him to leave Blefuscu.
8. Gulliver gets to England after his boat is picked up by an English ship returning to England from Japan.
9. Gulliver stays in England for two months before embarking on his second voyage.
10. Gulliver is enabled to go on his second voyage without leaving his family unsupported financially because he inherits an estate from his uncle.

Suggested Essay Topics

1. Discuss the total collapse of Gulliver's position in Lilliput and its causes.
2. Discuss Gulliver's disillusionment with politics.
3. Discuss the literary techniques by which Swift describes in a relatively few pages Gulliver's transition from condemned criminal in Lilliput to returned traveler in England.
4. Discuss elements of political satire, satire of the human condition, and satire of the traveler's tale in these chapters.

SECTION THREE

Part II: A Voyage to Brobdingnag

Chapters 1 and 2

New Characters:

The Farmer's Servant: *the giant Brobdingnagian, who picks up Gulliver and takes him to his master*

The Farmer: *Brobdingnagian who exhibits Gulliver as a curiosity*

The Farmer's Wife: *at first disgusted by Gulliver as though he were a spider, later sympathetic to him*

Glumdalclitch: *meaning "little nurse" in Brobdingnagian; the farmer's daughter, whose pet Gulliver becomes, and who continues to take care of him after he is bought by the Queen of Brobdingnag*

Summary

Gulliver sails for India (specifically Surat), but his ship is blown off course by a storm; an island is discovered, and Gulliver and some other men go to the island in one of the ship's boats. Gulliver walks toward the interior of the island, but he suddenly sees the other men running toward the ship's boat. They row out to the ship, leaving

Gulliver behind; they are being chased by a "huge creature." Gulliver flees and sees giant plants and then a man as tall as a church steeple. He and other giants are reaping enormous crops; he realizes that he is now in the same position with respect to these giants as the Lilliputians had been with respect to him. One of the reapers literally picks Gulliver up, puts him in his pocket, and takes him to the farmer whose servant he is. Gulliver again cooperates, as he had done in Lilliput. He steps into the farmer's handkerchief and frightens the farmer's wife, who is disgusted as if Gulliver were a spider. Later she becomes sympathetic to him. Gulliver sees the farmer's family, including three children and an old grandmother. He refuses to be frightened by the farmer's cat, although the animal seems to Gulliver to be three times the size of an ox. Gulliver sees the ugliness of people seen, in effect, at very close range, because they are gigantic from his viewpoint. He fights with Brobdingnagian rats.

In Chapter Two, Gulliver describes the farmer's daughter, who takes care of him. She calls him "Grildrig," or mannikin, while he calls her "Glimdalclitch," or little nurse in the Brobdingnagian language. Gulliver learns more of the language, and hears that the farmer intends to exhibit Gulliver for money as a public spectacle, which saddens Gulliver. His master takes Gulliver in a box to the neighboring town, where he does tricks before about thirty people at a time. He is later taken to the capital of the kingdom to be shown to the people there.

Analysis

The second voyage begins with an account of Gulliver's trip by sea, in which nautical language is used for humorous purposes. Swift returns to a plainer style and uses the difference in scale—here reversed since the people Gulliver sees are much larger than he is, rather than smaller—with impressive effect. Gulliver again cooperates with his captors, more understandable than in Lilliput, since he is now in the hands of people who are much larger than he is. His smallness humiliates him, and the ugliness of the human body as viewed in a magnified form provides Swift with another opportunity to satirize human frailty. Gulliver's self-esteem is again brought down. Swift is using Gulliver as an example of a typical human being and in effect commenting on human frailty and the futility of human wishes. In Brobdingnag, the only reason he is not crushed to death by the giant inhabitants is because he is a curiosity. He is unable to do the services that caused him to rise to high office, although temporarily, in Lilliput.

Thus human weaknesses are satirized by Swift in another way; they will continue to be so satirized in different ways throughout *Gulliver's Travels.*

Study Questions

1. How does Gulliver get to Brobdingnag?
2. Why is he abandoned by his shipmates there?
3. Who picks him up?
4. Where is he taken?
5. How do people of gigantic size appear to Gulliver?
6. How does Gulliver struggle with Brobdingnagian animals?
7. Who in Brobdingnag befriends him most closely?
8. What does the farmer plan to do with Gulliver?
9. Why does Gulliver dislike the farmer's plans?
10. Where is Gulliver taken toward the end of Chapter Two?

Answers

1. Gulliver gets to Brobdingnag because his ship is blown off course.
2. Gulliver's shipmates escape without him from Brobdingnag because they are frightened by the giants there.
3. The farmer's servant literally picks up Gulliver.
4. The farmer's servant takes Gulliver to the farmer.
5. To Gulliver, people of gigantic size appear ugly, since their bodily flaws are immensely magnified.
6. Gulliver refuses to be frightened by the farmer's cat and fights a bloody battle with Brobdingnagian rats.
7. The farmer's daughter, known to Gulliver as Glumdalclitch,

or "little nurse," is the Brobdingnagian who befriends Gulliver most closely.

8. The farmer plans to publicly exhibit Gulliver for money.
9. Gulliver feels insulted by the idea of being exhibited as a curiosity.
10. Toward the end of Chapter Two, the farmer takes Gulliver in a box to the capital city of Brobdingnag.

Suggested Essay Topics

1. Discuss the way Swift uses the difference of scale between Gulliver and the Brobdingnagians to literary effect.
2. Discuss the way changes in tone advance the narrative in the first two chapters of Gulliver's second voyage.
3. How does Swift ironically comment on human frailty in these chapters? Discuss.
4. Discuss the changes in Gulliver's relationships with the Brobdingnagians in these chapters.

Chapters 3 and 4

New Characters:

The Queen of Brobdingnag: *buys Gulliver from the farmer and presents him to the King*

The King: *ruler of Brobdingnag, a patron of scholarship; asks Gulliver to describe England to him*

The Queen's Dwarf: *becomes Gulliver's enemy because he is no longer the smallest person at court*

Summary

A gentleman usher commands Gulliver's master to bring him to the royal court for the entertainment of the Queen of Brobdingnag and the royal ladies. Gulliver expresses willingness to be sold to the Queen, and the farmer sells him to her. Gulliver then asks that

Glumdalclitch continue as his nurse, and this is agreed to. Gulliver meets the King of Brobdingnag, a great scholar and patron of learning. Gulliver is examined by three great scholars, who, after examining him, pronounce Gulliver a sport of nature, a concept used by modern philosophy, according to Swift, to explain things that in an earlier time would have been explained by occult causes. The King asks the farmer and Glumdalclitch about Gulliver; the latter is appointed a regular member of the royal household, and a house and furniture are built for Gulliver. Clothing and plates are also made for him, and ladies of the court amuse themselves by watching Gulliver eat.

The King asks Gulliver detailed questions about Europe and its manners and government. He then laughingly asks Gulliver whether he is a Whig or Tory, reflecting that such small creatures also have their titles, customs, houses, and the like. The Queen's dwarf, no longer being the smallest person at court, becomes Gulliver's enemy and throws him into a bowl of cream. Glumdalclitch rescues Gulliver and the dwarf is punished. Gulliver fights giant insects.

In Chapter Four, Gulliver gives a description of Brobdingnag, which he traveled around with the royal court. The palace, for example, is a heap of buildings seven miles around, with the main rooms two hundred and forty feet high. Gulliver sees gigantic lice on peoples' clothes and is revolted. He is carried around in a traveling closet.

Analysis

Swift continues to attract the reader's sympathy for Gulliver, who is virtually powerless in Brobdingnag because of his small size. The king ironically comments that the miserably small English have their organized society, as if he were discussing a colony of ants or a beehive. Gulliver is ashamed. He is almost powerless against the thirty-foot court dwarf and has to be rescued by Glumdalclitch. His revulsion at gigantic people, whose physical defects and insect parasites are clearly visible to him, indicates an aspect of Swift's view of human beings; from certain viewpoints, we are disgusting.

The description of the Kingdom of Brobdingnag in Chapter Four is based almost entirely on the discrepancy in scale and is comparable to certain parts of the description of Lilliput in the first volume.

The Brobdingnagians are more generous to Gulliver than the Lilliputians; in a non-literal way they are also "big people," while the Lilliputians are "little people."

His continuing danger from gigantic animals and insects also emphasizes the theme of Gulliver's smallness in Brobdingnag. Swift, the clergyman, is perhaps also implying the insignificance of human beings compared to the immense majesty of God, a theme expressed in another way in the voyage to Lilliput, where the political schemes and the like of the inhabitants seem small and contemptible to Gulliver, at least toward the end of his journey.

In none of his journeys is Gulliver a conqueror, in contrast to many of the authors of travel books popular in Swift's time. Of course, Swift himself in 1726 was in Dublin, far from the center of things in London, where he had lived previously; he was also no longer young, and Vanessa had died three years earlier, so that autobiographical elements are also present under the surface.

Study Questions

1. To whom does the farmer sell Gulliver?
2. What does the King of Brobdingnag discuss with Gulliver?
3. What do the Brobdingnagian philosophers think Gulliver is?
4. What does the King of Brobdingnag think of England?
5. How does Gulliver react to the King's comments on England?
6. Who is Gulliver's enemy at the court of Brobdingnag?
7. How large is the palace of Brobdingnag, according to Gulliver?
8. How is Gulliver transported around the kingdom?
9. What is the most hateful sight in Brobdingnag, according to Gulliver?
10. What insects bother Gulliver in Brobdingnag?

Answers

1. The farmer sells Gulliver to the Queen of Brobdingnag.
2. The King of Brobdingnag discusses the customs and institutions of England with Gulliver.
3. The Brobdingnagian philosophers think Gulliver is a sport of nature.
4. The King of Brobdingnag thinks that the small size of the English shows how contemptible human pretensions are, since they have titles of honor political parties, and the like.
5. Gulliver reacts at first with resentment at the King's attitude toward England, but then realizes that he himself would seem ridiculous to someone so many times larger than he was.
6. Gulliver's enemy at the court of Brobdingnag is the Dwarf, who resents no longer being the smallest person at court.
7. According to Gulliver, the palace of Brobdingnag is a heap of buildings seven miles around.
8. Gulliver is transported around the kingdom in a box (actually there were two boxes of different sizes).
9. The most hateful sight in Brobdingnag, according to Gulliver, was that of gigantic lice on peoples' bodies.
10. Gulliver is bothered in Brobdingnag by gigantic flies.

Suggested Essay Topics

1. Discuss the attitude of the King of Brobdingnag to England, and Gulliver's attitude toward it, as satire of human frailty.
2. How does the description of Brobdingnag in Chapter Four use the difference in scale between Gulliver and the Brobdingnagians? Discuss.
3. How does Gulliver's trouble with the dwarf satirize human frailty?
4. How do Chapters Three and Four deepen the reader's understanding of Brobdingnag in general? Discuss.

Chapters 5 and 6

New Characters:

The Maids of Honor: *play with Gulliver and undress in his presence, which he finds disgusting because of their immense size*

Summary

Gulliver continues to be tormented by the Dwarf, is pelted by Brobdingnagian hailstones, is picked up by a dog but rescued by a gardener, and is attacked again by birds.

Glumdalclitch and Gulliver are frequently invited by the Maids of Honor of the court to their rooms. They would strip him naked and lay him full length on their bosoms. Gulliver is offended by their odor; similarly a Lilliputian had once told him that he was offended by Gulliver's odor. The Maids of Honor undress in Gulliver's presence, which Gulliver finds offensive. Gulliver witnesses an execution, rows a boat, and almost falls forty feet on the floor. He is attacked by a frog and a monkey, who puts him on the roof of a building, but is rescued by men with ladders. He describes his close escape from death to the King, who finds it amusing. Gulliver feels like a poor man attempting to mix with the rich.

In Chapter Six, Gulliver watches the King being shaved, and he makes a comb out of bristles of the King's hair and some pieces of wood. He makes pieces cut from the Queen's hair into furniture. He tries to play a spinet (piano-like instrument) sixty feet long. He gives a detailed description of England to the King, who ridicules political corruption there. The King ridicules the idea of figuring the population of England based on the numbers of members of various religious sects, saying that people with dangerous religious opinions ought to hide them.

The King also ridicules gambling and political violence in England. He says that on the basis of Gulliver's description of his country, "the bulk" of the English are "the most pernicious race of odious little vermin that Nature ever suffered (allowed) to crawl upon the surface of the earth."

Analysis

Here Swift again emphasizes human frailty in the form of Gulliver's constantly precarious situation among the giant Brobdingnagians, whose birds, dogs, and monkeys are a threat to him. The same theme appears, expressed in a different way, when the disgusting nature of human beings, when magnified, offends Gulliver. In other words, looked at from certain viewpoints, we are all disgusting because of our human imperfections.

The theme of human frailty and imperfection is expressed in still another way in the King's reaction to Gulliver's patriotic description of his native land. English politics, with its normal human frailty, seems to be that of "odious little vermin" to the King, who is gigantic in every sense. Looked at from the viewpoint of a superior outsider, with "Olympian detachment," a term originally applied to the imagined viewpoint of the ancient Greek gods who lived on Mount Olympus according to mythology, human society seems to be almost literally a "rat race."

The King of Brobdingnag is the most sympathetic human character, in fact the most sympathetic character, in the entire book. He is "big," just as the Emperor of Lilliput is "small." He is the ideal Tory king, the father of his country, although perhaps he is insufficiently tolerant of the frailty of a foreign country. His kingdom is no Utopia, having poverty, disease, envy, and vanity, but it is better than England. There is less corruption, and good laws rather than unenforceable Utopian laws.

Here we have Swift's view of the best society humanly possible. The King of Brobdingnag is not, unlike most of the characters of *Gulliver's Travels*, viewed from an ironic perspective. He may in fact be viewed as the true hero of the work, unlike the basically good but naive and often unwise Gulliver. If Gulliver is Swift's idea of the average person (the way people really are), the King of Brobdingnag is the superior person (the way people should be). The King is not perfect, since to Swift, in accordance with his Christian beliefs, no human being can be perfect in this world, but he is as close to perfect as anyone can be in this imperfect (imperfect since Adam ate the apple, as Swift, the Anglican clergyman, believed) world.

Study Questions

1. What do the Maids of Honor do in front of Gulliver and why?
2. How does their action affect him?
3. How does Gulliver escape from a monkey?
4. What is the King's reaction to Gulliver's escape?
5. How does Gulliver react to the King's reaction?
6. What does Gulliver do after watching the King of Brobdingnag shave?
7. How does Gulliver try to perform musically in Brobdingnag?
8. What does the King of Brobdingnag think of Gulliver's description of England?
9. Why does he hold this attitude?
10. What is the King's attitude to religious freedom?

Answers

1. The Maids of Honor undress before Gulliver, not being ashamed any more than if he were a small animal.
2. Gulliver finds the magnified physical imperfections of the Maids disgusting.
3. Men with ladders are sent to the roof of a building to rescue Gulliver from the monkey.
4. The King thinks Gulliver's narrow escape from death at the hands of the monkey is amusing.
5. Gulliver feels, when the King is amused at Gulliver's account of his narrow escape, like an awkward social climber.
6. After watching the King shave, Gulliver uses some bristles of the King's hair and some wood splinters and makes a comb.
7. Gulliver tries to play a sixty-foot-long spinet (piano-like instrument).
8. The King of Brobdingnag, after hearing Gulliver's description of England, thinks, despite Gulliver's patriotism, that the

English are the "most pernicious race of odious little vermin that Nature ever suffered (allowed) to crawl upon the surface of the earth."

9. The King holds a very negative opinion of the English because of their political and moral corruption.
10. The King thinks that people should hold harmful religious views in private only, not in public.

Suggested Essay Topics

1. How, in these chapters, does Gulliver's sense of human frailty deepen? Discuss.
2. Discuss the King of Brobdingnag's reactions to Gulliver's patriotic description of England.
3. Discuss the ways in which the King of Brobdingnag appears as the most sympathetic character in the book, in fact as an ideal king.
4. Compare and contrast the King of Brobdingnag's opinions of the human race and its frailties with the opinions of Gulliver.

Chapters 7 and 8

New Character:

Thomas Wilcocks: *English sea captain who rescues Gulliver and takes him back to England after the box in which he was carried in Brobdingnag falls into the sea; at first thinks Gulliver is crazy*

Summary

Gulliver continues to describe England, answering the King of Brobdingnag's questions; despite Gulliver's efforts to present England in the best possible light, the King sees the bad features. Gulliver tells the King about gunpowder, trying to instruct the king to have it made, together with firearms, but the Brobdingnagian King is aghast at the existence of so terrible a weapon. Gulliver

thinks that the King is unnecessarily cautious. The King is unfamiliar with European secrets of statecraft, and thinks that:

> whoever could make two ears of corn, or two blades of grass to grow upon a spot where only one grew before, would deserve better of mankind, and do more essential service to his country, than the whole race of politicians put together.

This is one of the most famous statements in Swift's works; Gulliver thinks the King "confined the knowledge of governing within very narrow bounds." In other words, the King seems to Gulliver to be naive.

Gulliver notes that the knowledge of the Brobdingnagians is practical, not theoretical; they explain things in very simple terms. To write a commentary on any law is punished by death; there are few crimes or legal disputes, anyway.

Their books are gigantic, to Gulliver, but the Brobdingnagians' style is clear. One book emphasizes the weakness of human beings.

The Brobdingnagians, observes Gulliver, have a large army, organized as a militia under the command of local landowners. Although there are no external armies, the army is large to prevent civil strife.

In Chapter Eight, Gulliver complains that he is well treated but not free in Brobdingnag. He had been in the country for two years when the King takes him along on a royal tour of the country, together with Glumdalclitch; Gulliver is carried in his box. When near the ocean, Gulliver is asleep in his box when he discovers that the box is raised very high in the air. In fact an eagle has picked him up, the ring attached to the box being in the bird's beak. The bird drops the box, which floats in the ocean. Gulliver is hoisted up. He has been picked up by an English ship; the carpenter saws a hole in the box and rescues Gulliver. Gulliver is confused because he is now among men his own size. The captain of the ship, Thomas Wilcocks, thinks Gulliver is crazy at first but later believes his story. He suggests that Gulliver write an account of his voyages; Gulliver thinks that there are already too many travel books.

Gulliver is taken back to England, has trouble adjusting to the scale, and is at first thought crazy by his family. His wife asks him never to go to sea again, but he does go.

Analysis

Again in these chapters, Swift employs variations on the theme of human frailty and imperfection. Irony is employed in displaying the naive Gulliver's viewing the greater humanity of the King of Brobdingnag as naiveté. Thinking that he is being helpful, Gulliver proposes the introduction of firearms to the King. The King is shocked at the use of such fearsome weapons; Gulliver thinks him naive. Again, Gulliver represents the average Englishman, while the King represents Swift's idea of the good king, a goodness the depraved Englishman mistakes for "narrowness." It is, however, true that Brobdingnag has no external enemies, or neighbors at all. The King represents a wise, relatively realistic, idealism, which is Swift's Tory and Christian ideal of government.

Brobdingnag's books avoid the unnecessarily theoretical; Gulliver, representing the average Englishman, sees this as naive primitivism. Swift, here employing dramatic irony, clearly sees this as wisdom. Swift, as a clergyman familiar with recent English history, is expressing his weariness with overly technical debates on the fine points of theology.

One Brobdingnagian book, "in little esteem except among the women and the vulgar," treats of human weakness and frailty; even among the giants, it seems, there is such a book.

The description of the militia represents Swift's Tory ideal of the territorial militia rather than the professional, standing army. There are no external enemies, but an army is necessary to prevent civil war. England had, of course, experienced civil strife in the seventeenth century, and the hated Oliver Cromwell had temporarily introduced a standing army.

In Chapter Eight, when Gulliver has been in Brobdingnag for two years and is afraid he will be kept there like a pet animal for the rest of his life, he is rescued by a *deus ex machina*. This term, from the Latin, literally means "god from the machine." It refers back to ancient plays in which a figure representing a god suddenly appears on stage, having been brought in by machinery, and rescues the main character or otherwise solves the problem which had prevented the play from ending in a satisfactory manner. Here the *deus ex machina* is an eagle, who picks up Gulliver in his box and drops him into the sea, where he is picked up by an English ship.

In contrast to the situation in Lilliput, Gulliver is allowed to escape by pure chance, not by any act on his own part, as might be expected in a land of giants. On the way to England, and back home, he has trouble adjusting to the change of scale, creating opportunities for both irony and humor for Swift. A normal person might, after such experiences, never want to leave home again, but not the sympathetically naive Gulliver. By this time, the reader sympathizes with Gulliver because of his innocence.

Study Questions

1. Why does Gulliver tell the King of Brobdingnag about gunpowder?
2. What is the King's reaction to what Gulliver tells him about gunpowder and firearms?
3. What does Gulliver think of the King of Brobdingnag's ideas about government?
4. What are the Brobdingnagian books like according to Gulliver?
5. What is the Brobdingnagian army like according to him?
6. Why do they have an army, since there are no external enemies?
7. Why is Gulliver unhappy at the beginning of Chapter Eight?
8. Where is Gulliver when he is about to leave Brobdingnag?
9. How does he leave Brobdingnag?
10. How does he return to England?

Answers

1. Gulliver is trying to help the King of Brobdingnag to defend his kingdom by telling him about gunpowder and firearms.
2. The King is shocked that brutally destructive weapons such as firearms exist.
3. Gulliver thinks that the King of Brobdingnag's idealistic ideas about government are narrow, meaning naive.

4. Brobdingnagian books, according to Gulliver, are gigantic, direct, practical and not theoretical.
5. Gulliver tells the reader that the Brobdingnagian army is a militia, in which the commanders are local landowners.
6. The Brobdingnagians have an army, despite the lack of external enemies, to prevent civil strife.
7. At the beginning of Chapter Eight, Gulliver is unhappy because he is afraid that he will spend the rest of his life being treated like a poor animal by the Brobdingnagians.
8. When he is about to leave Brobdingnag, Gulliver is at the seashore.
9. Gulliver is picked up in his box by an eagle and dropped in the sea.
10. Gulliver is picked up by an English ship in which he is taken back to England.

Suggested Essay Topics

1. Compare Gulliver's political views, as stated in these chapters, with those of the King of Brobdingnag.
2. In what way do Brobdingnagian books display Swift's ideals? Compare these ideals with the beliefs Swift puts in the mouth of Gulliver. Discuss.
3. The Brobdingnagian army is organized according to Swift's political views. Discuss.
4. In what way does Gulliver's return to England represent the third voyage's repeated emphasis on human frailty? Discuss.

SECTION FOUR

Part III: A Voyage to Laputa, Balnibarbi, Glubbdubdrib, Luggnag, and Japan

Chapters 1, 2, and 3

New Characters:

Captain William Robinson: *invites Gulliver on his third voyage*

The Dutchman: *one of the pirates who attack Gulliver's ship; proposes that Gulliver be set adrift*

The Japanese Pirate: *sets Gulliver adrift*

The King of the Flying Island of Laputa: *interested only in mathematics, science, and astronomy; asks Gulliver only about these subjects*

Summary

Ten days after his arrival in England from his second voyage, Gulliver is asked by Captain William Robinson to be ship's surgeon, on a voyage to the East Indies, in two months. He persuades his wife, after some difficulties, to allow him to go. After spending time in India and Tonquin (part of modern Vietnam), Gulliver's ship is driven off course by a storm and attacked by pirate ships. Gulliver antagonizes a Dutch pirate by telling him that Gulliver and his men are Christians. The Dutch pirate tries to persuade the Japanese captain of the larger pirate ship to throw him into the sea; instead, Gulliver is set adrift in a small boat. He sails to a small island; after sailing to several islands, Gulliver lands on an island and is surprised to see an immense object in the sky. It turns out to be an island in the air, inhabited by people, with several levels and stairways. Gulliver asks for help with gestures, and he is pulled up to the island.

In Chapter Two, Gulliver sees people attended by servants, called "flappers," who gently hit them with balloon-like objects filled with dry peas or small pebbles to rouse them when they are deep in thought, which is usually the case.

Gulliver visits the King and attends a banquet in which the foods are cut in the shape of geometrical figures and musical instruments. Clothing is similarly decorated, and is also decorated with figures of suns, moons, and stars. After Gulliver learns some of the language, he has clothes made for him. The tailors measure his body with navigational instruments and make mathematical calculations; the resulting garments are, as is common in Laputa, very ill-fitting. The Laputans hear the music of the spheres, pick up petitions from the land below with pack-threads and weights, praise people and animals in geometric terms, and in general are very theoretically oriented and bad at practical matters. They believe in astrology, and the men are often cheated on by their wives. The women favor men from the land below the island, because they are bored by their excessively theoretical and impractical husbands. The King has no interest in the general state of things in England, asking Gulliver only about mathematics there.

In Chapter Three, Gulliver learns that the Flying or Floating Island is exactly circular, contains ten thousand acres, can be raised above the clouds, and is enabled to fly by a gigantic magnetic stone in a chasm in the island's center. The island cannot fly away from the land beneath, nor can it fly above a four-mile altitude. It is steered by astronomers, who have also discovered two additional satellites of Mars.

Rebellions are put down by having the island hover over the rebellious area, cutting off sunlight. If necessary, the islanders fight by bombarding the rebels from above with rocks. One rebellious city won concessions by building towers with magnetic stones at each of the city's four corners, preventing countermeasures by the King of the Floating Island.

Analysis

Swift depicts here the book's only realm run by normal-sized human beings. In order to keep up the fantastic tone of the book, he introduces other science-fiction type devices. As usual, Gulliver meets with disaster on the way to unknown parts; pirates capture his ship, and the Dutch pirate is far harsher to Gulliver than the Japanese pirate ship captain. In his political writings, Swift argues that in the War of the Spanish Succession, in progress in 1707, which is the dramatic date at the beginning of this voyage, the Dutch were unfaithful allies to England against France.

The Laputans, absorbed to the point of distraction in theoretical speculations, represent a satire of certain intellectual tendencies in Swift's time—the beginning of the "Age of Reason" and the "Scientific Revolution." The Royal Society, the first scientific society in the world, had been chartered in 1662, five years before Swift's birth. Swift had satirized excessively theoretical, impractical thinkers in earlier writings. In these respects, the Laputans are the exact opposite of the Brobdingnagians, who are eager to learn from others' experience, are strong in practical matters and weaker in theoretical matters. Thus, the King of Brobdingnag is very interested in Gulliver's account of England, while the ruler in Laputa is interested only in mathematics there. The Lilliputians had no interest in England.

To Gulliver with his Tory mindset, the flying island symbolizes the royal court of a country such as England. The mainland below represents the country at large; they are dependent on each other. The land below may also be interpreted as Ireland, which is "below" England, that is, under English rule. The danger is that the rulers may be so preoccupied by matters of theory, perhaps theological and political, that they neglect practical politics.

In this section, Gulliver is among people his own size. He is neither a victorious general nor a freak under display, but a mere spectator, a foreign tourist, like Swift himself in his early days in England.

Study Questions

1. How does Gulliver get to Laputa?
2. How does Laputa differ from a normal country?
3. How do the people differ from those in most countries?
4. What unusual kind of servants do the better-off Laputans have?
5. What is unusual about Laputan food and clothing?
6. What does the King of Laputa ask Gulliver about England?
7. What makes the island fly?
8. How do the Laputans put down rebellions?
9. What have Laputan astronomers discovered?
10. How were rebels successful in one case against Laputa?

Answers

1. Gulliver gets to Laputa after being cast adrift on a small boat by pirates who have captured his ship.
2. Laputa is a flying or floating island, moving above the ground.
3. The Laputans are almost totally absorbed in abstract speculation, to the neglect of practical activities.
4. The better-off Laputans have servants called "flappers." Their servants gently hit them with balloon-like objects filled with dried peas or pebbles so they will not be totally distracted in thought from the outside world.
5. Laputan food is shaped like geometrical figures or musical instruments and their clothing is similarly decorated. Their clothing is also decorated with astronomical figures. Clothing is made and fitted using navigational instruments and mathematical calculations, and it is ill-fitting.
6. The King of Laputa asks Gulliver about the state of mathematics in England; he is interested in nothing else about England.

7. A magnetic rock in a cave in the center of the island of Laputa makes it fly.
8. The Laputans put down rebellions by flying over the rebellious area, blocking out sunlight, and if necessary throwing down rocks.
9. Laputan astronomers have discovered two additional satellites of Mars.
10. Rebels against Laputa were able to get favorable terms by putting magnetic towers at the four corners of their city, defeating Laputan measures against them.

Suggested Essay Topics

1. Discuss the various devices Swift uses to convey the excessively theoretical, impractical, nature of Laputan society.
2. Although Laputa is depicted negatively by Swift, the Laputans have made some positive discoveries. Discuss.
3. How do Gulliver's activities in Laputa differ from those on his first two voyages? Discuss.
4. Discuss political satire in these chapters.

Chapters 4, 5, and 6

New Characters:

The Court Official: *related to the King of Laputa; intervenes with the King to allow Gulliver to leave the Flying Island for Balnibarbi, the continent on the ground beneath it*

The Lord Munodi: *official, former governor of Lagado; describes the continent to Gulliver; shows him the Academy*

First Scholar: *member of the Academy of Lagado; tries to extract sunbeams from cucumbers*

Second Scholar: *tries to reduce human excrement to its original food*

Architect: *tries to build houses from the top down*

Blind Artists: *leads apprentices, also blind, trying to mix paint colors by smell*

Projector: *tries to plow the ground with hogs*

Artist: *tries to use spiders as silkworms*

Physician: *tries to cure people by pumping them with a bellows*

Universal Artist: *tries a variety of impossible experiments*

Speculative Professor: *makes a frame with all the words in the Lagadan language written on pieces of wood; composes nonsensical literary works by rearranging them at random*

Language Professors: *try to substitute images of things discussed for words, eliminating the necessity of speaking*

Mathematical Professor: *tries to teach by giving students pills to take, containing knowledge*

Political Professor: *tries to cure politicians by medicine and violence*

Second and Third Political Professors: *propose absurd methods of taxation*

Fourth Political Professor: *tries to discover conspiracies against the government by studying people's food*

Summary

Gulliver, tired of the Floating Island, befriends a court official, related to the King, who intervenes to allow Gulliver to depart. Gulliver receives money from the King and a recommendation from the official to a friend of his in Lagado, capital of the mainland continent of Balnibarbi. Gulliver lands and gives the letter to the official's friend the Lord Munodi, former governor of Lagado. Balnibarbi is a poor country. Munodi is polite and describes the continent to Gulliver, showing him the Academy of Lagado, founded some years before by people who had returned from several months in the Floating Island with a smattering of mathematics, "but full of volatile spirits acquired in that airy region."

The Academy uses theoretical knowledge to bring about what its members believe to be great improvements and inventions, none of which have been perfected. In the meantime, other activities being neglected, the country has become very poor. Munodi, like a few other local lords, was content to live in the old, time-honored way. He was exempt from the poverty prevalent elsewhere on the continent, but was attacked as lazy.

In Chapter Five, Gulliver visits and describes the Academy of Lagado, which is not one building but several houses along a street.

The first scholar Gulliver sees in the Academy has been working for eight years on a project for extracting sunbeams from cucumbers. The second had long been trying in vain to reduce human excrement to its original food. An architect is trying to build houses from the top down. A man born blind is, aided by blind assistants, trying to mix paint colors by smell. Another tries to plow the ground with hogs; another tries to use spiders as silkworms. An astronomer tries to put a sundial on a weathervane and a physician tries to cure patients by pumping them with a bellows. There are others involved in similar vain, extravagant schemes.

A "universal artist" directs a workshop in which 50 men are involved in a variety of fantastic experiments, such as softening marble for pillows and pincushions and breeding naked sheep without wool.

Gulliver then visits the more theoretically oriented part of the Academy, where he sees a professor who has had a 20-foot square frame made and placed in the center of the room. The frame is filled with many small pieces of wood linked together by thin wires, each being labeled with a word, so that all the words in the language in all grammatical forms appear on the frame. By manipulating the frame, the words are moved around. They sometimes form incomplete sentences, which the professor wants to piece together to form literary works. Other language professors want people to carry objects representing all things instead of speaking. Another professor tries to teach mathematics by having students take pills containing knowledge.

At the beginning of Chapter Six, Gulliver visits the school of political projectors. The projectors are trying the impossibly idealistic scheme of getting kings to choose officials on the basis of their wisdom, abilities, and virtues rather than their connections. Other professors there try to cure politicians of their imperfections by medicines and violent attacks, or through transplanting part of the brains of some politicians into the heads of others. Other professors propose taxing such things as vices and compliments, or taxing women on their beauty and skill in dressing. Others propose that public offices should be raffled off, while another proposes to discover plots against the government by studying peoples' food.

Gulliver proposes that the Academy adopt a plan used in "Tribnia" (anagram of Britain). People should be arrested and, through deliberate misinterpretation of their letters they should be accused of using secret codes in fantastic ways. Thus "our brother Tom has got the piles," is suspected to be code for "Resist; a plot is brought home, the tour." Gulliver is commended for his suggestion, but decides to return to England.

Analysis

Gulliver is satirizing impractical, visionary scientific experiments and theories, such as the Royal Society was proposing. The political projectors are proposing, in a ridiculous way, tyrannical police-state methods, possibly similar to the excesses of Sir Robert Walpole's intelligence service, which according to many people was fabricating evidence against people accused of trying to restore the Stuart dynasty to the English throne. The impracticality on the continent results from insufficient mathematical knowledge combined with an extremely theoretical orientation acquired from the Floating Island. Gulliver continues to satirize the neglect of practical, down-to-earth tasks, which causes poverty. As a Tory, he is also satirizing neglect of traditional methods of doing things in favor of visionary speculation and hinting that this speculation can be turned to the support of tyranny. Undoubtedly, English rule of Ireland was one of the things being satirized, but not the only thing Swift had in mind.

The idea of reducing words to mere "things" and making them measurable on a machine was also offensive to Swift's Christian religious beliefs. To some Christians, "the Word is God." Misguided science can thus be brought into the service of tyranny and irreligion. The contrast with the more practically oriented society of Brobdingnag should also be kept in mind throughout the third voyage. Gulliver, reduced to a mere observer, wants to leave, not because he is a prisoner, which he is not on this voyage, but merely because

he is bored. The implication is that theoretical speculation of this kind is arid and thus dull. It is artificial to the point of inhumanity.

Study Questions

1. How does Gulliver leave the Floating Island?
2. How did the Academy of Lagado originate?
3. What are the consequences of establishing the Academy?
4. What, generally, does the Academy of Lagado do?
5. What is the first scholar Gulliver sees at the Academy of Lagado trying to do?
6. What is the architect Gulliver sees at the Academy trying to do?
7. What is the first physician Gulliver sees at the Academy attempting?
8. What is the first activity Gulliver sees in the more theoretically oriented part of the Academy?
9. What are the political professors doing to cure politicians?
10. What does Gulliver propose to the Academy of Lagado?

Answers

1. Gulliver leaves the Floating Island by getting a court official, related to the King, to intervene.
2. The Academy of Lagado originated when some people from the continent of Balnibarbi spent some months on the Floating Island, learning a little mathematics but filling themselves with "volatile spirits," meaning impractical, theoretical orientation (not liquor).
3. The consequence of the Academy is poverty, caused by the neglect of practical work in favor of visionary, impracticable, schemes.
4. The Academy of Lagado comes up with a variety of visionary, impracticable schemes that have not yet been perfected (and presumably never will be).

5. The first scholar Gulliver sees at the Academy of Lagado has been working for eight years on a project for extracting sunbeams from cucumbers.
6. The architect Gulliver first sees at the Academy is trying to build houses from the top down.
7. The first physician Gulliver sees at the Academy is trying to cure patients with a bellows.
8. The first activity Gulliver sees in the more theoretically oriented part of the Academy is an attempt to create new writings by putting all the words of the language on pieces of wood, linked by wires, on an enormous frame and rearranging them mechanically.
9. The politicians are trying to cure professors with medicines and violent attacks, or through brain transplants.
10. Gulliver proposes to the Academy of Lagado a scheme to accuse people of plots against the state by misinterpreting their letters as secret codes.

Suggested Essay Topics

1. The Academy of Lagado suggests that Swift thinks "a little knowledge is a dangerous thing." Discuss.
2. Discuss the way the Academy of Lagado satirizes political events in England and Ireland in Swift's time.
3. Discuss the Academy of Lagado as a satire of intellectual tendencies in Swift's time.
4. Discuss how the satire of the Academy of Lagado relates to Swift's vocation as an Anglican clergyman.

Chapters 7, 8 and 9

New Characters:

Governor of Glubbdubdrib: *has ghosts for servants; acts as host to Gulliver; calls up spirits of famous historical figures at Gulliver's request*

Custom-House Officer: *confines Gulliver in Luggnag*

King of Luggnag: *acts as Gulliver's host; invites Gulliver to stay permanently, but he refuses*

Summary

Gulliver travels to the port of Maldonada, to get a ship to Luggnag, a country which trades with Japan. There being no ship available for some time, Gulliver makes a side-trip to the small island of Glubbdubdrib, the island of sorcerers or magicians. The people are all magicians, and when Gulliver is received by the Governor of the island, he finds that, as he had heard, the Governor's servants are ghosts. The Governor lets Gulliver call up the ghosts of anyone he chooses; Gulliver sees many famous people, mostly from classical antiquity. He prefers to see the destroyers of tyrants and usurpers, and restorers of liberty to their people.

In Chapter Eight, Gulliver sees the ghosts of Homer and Aristotle, famous philosophers and Roman Emperors. Gulliver finds out that most kings are actually of humble descent. He discovers that historians have falsified history to make people look morally better, and to hide the extent of human corruption, including the sins of most holders of high office. Gulliver discovers that in ancient Rome the deserving went without rewards and the undeserving were rewarded. Only the old English yeoman was apparently exempt from corruption.

In Chapter Nine, Gulliver finally goes to Luggnag, where he is kept confined by a custom-house officer. The King sends for Gulliver, who has to lick the dust before the royal footstool. The King punishes people by poisoning the dust they have to lick. Gulliver stays with the Court of Luggnag for three months, turning down offers to remain there permanently.

Analysis

Swift's merciless attacks on human frailty continue unrelentingly; the ghosts prove that corruption and unfairness are far from new. Swift is in the tradition of visits to the dead in Homer, Virgil, and Dante. Although there is praise for liberators and the old English yeoman, the continuing emphasis on human frailty and corruption bores even Gulliver, who in this voyage is mostly a mere spectator. This emphasis on human failings has caused Swift to be accused of misanthropy (hatred of human beings in general). There is also some feeling against monarchy in general expressed in these chapters, which is rather strange for an Anglican Tory.

Study Questions

1. Why does Gulliver visit Glubbdubdrib?
2. What kind of place is it?
3. Who are the Governor's servants in Glubbdubdrib?
4. What is Gulliver allowed to do in Glubbdubdrib?
5. Who are some of the famous people Gulliver sees in Glubbdubdrib?
6. What does Gulliver learn from the philosophers there?
7. What does Gulliver learn about kings and rulers there?
8. Who are the sympathetic figures in Glubbdubdrib?
9. What does Gulliver have to do in the Court of Luggnag?
10. How are people sometimes punished there?

Answers

1. Gulliver visits Glubbdubdrib because he is delayed on the way to Luggnag.
2. Glubbdubdrib is a country of magicians.
3. The Governor's servants are ghosts.
4. Gulliver is allowed to call up the ghosts of whomever he pleases and ask them questions.
5. In Glubbdubdrib, Gulliver sees the ghosts of many famous people, including Homer, Aristotle, and Roman Emperors.
6. Gulliver learns from the philosophers at Glubbdubdrib (or rather from their ghosts) that commentators have misinterpreted their writings.
7. Gulliver learns that kings and rulers are corrupt, and were usually of humble origin a few generations back.

8. The sympathetic figures among the ghosts in Glubbdubdrib are the destroyers of tyrants and usurpers, the restorers of liberty to their people, and the old, honest, sincere English yeomen (small farmers).
9. In the Court of Luggnag, Gulliver has to lick the dust before the King's footstool.
10. In Luggnag, people are sometimes punished by having the dust they lick poisoned.

Suggested Essay Topics

1. Discuss the use of history to emphasize human frailty in these chapters.
2. Discuss Gulliver's political ideals in these chapters.
3. Discuss Swift's philosophical and literary ideals as indicated by his account of the ghosts of philosophers and authors in Luggnag.
4. Discuss weariness on Gulliver's part in these chapters and the reasons for it.

Chapters 10 and 11

New Characters:

Struldbruggs: *immortal Laggnagians who lack eternal youth and are therefore unable to do much or remember anything.*

Emperor of Japan: *suspects Gulliver of being a Christian after he refuses to trample on a crucifix.*

Summary

At Luggnag, Gulliver is told that some people born there are Struldbruggs or Immortals. Gulliver is, at first, impressed by the idea of people who live forever and are therefore able to bring the experience of the ages to each generation. Then he discovers that they have only eternal life and not eternal youth, and are thus unable to do much or remember anything. They are despised and hated, having to be supported at public expense.

Gulliver finally travels to Japan, where he is told that, like the Dutch who trade with the Japanese, he has to publicly trample on a crucifix in order to be allowed to leave. With some difficulty, he is exempted from this requirement, although this exemption has to be kept secret from the Dutch. The Japanese Emperor suspects Gulliver of being a Christian. Gulliver passes as a Dutchman, and he goes to the Netherlands on a Dutch ship. From there he returns to England, finding his family in good health.

Analysis

The Struldbruggs disappoint Gulliver by having eternal life and not eternal youth, defeating what Gulliver thinks would be the very purpose of immortality. Gulliver is satirizing travelers' tales about immortals by using a very old theme from Greek mythology, eternal life without eternal youth. Swift himself, it should be remembered, was almost sixty when *Gulliver's Travels* was written. Gulliver is depicted as naive in thinking that the Struldbruggs have eternal youth as well as eternal life. To the clergyman Swift, the only true eternal life is that promised by Christianity.

This section contains one of the book's few explicit references to Christianity. Gulliver's refusal to trample on the crucifix in Japan and the Emperor's suspicion that he might be a Christian are both significant. The anti-Dutch theme continues. In Swift's time, Japan—the only real country in the titles of Gulliver's four voyages, and the only non-European country described with any degree of detail—was deliberately cut off from the outside world. This was done partially to keep Christianity out of Japan. Only the Dutch were allowed to trade with Japan, to a very limited degree. They have to trample on the crucifix to show they are not Christian missionaries and to humiliate themselves. The crucifix is a symbol of Catholicism, and the Dutch were mostly Protestants.

Study Questions

1. Who are the Struldbruggs?
2. What misconception does Gulliver have about them?
3. Why does Gulliver, under a misconception, think of the Struldbruggs?
4. What are the Struldbruggs really like?
5. What is the attitude of other people toward them?
6. What is one of the reasons for this attitude?
7. How does Gulliver get to Japan?
8. To whom is Gulliver taken in Japan?
9. What does Gulliver ask not to have to do?
10. How does Gulliver get back to England?

Answers

1. The Struldbruggs are people in Luggnag who have eternal life but not eternal youth.
2. Gulliver does not realize that the Struldbruggs lack eternal youth.
3. Gulliver thinks that the Struldbruggs are able to use their wisdom and experience to enlighten younger generations.
4. The Struldbruggs, lacking eternal youth, are unable to do much or remember anything.
5. Other people hate and despise the Struldbruggs.
6. The Struldbruggs are hated and despised partly because they have to be supported at public expense.
7. Gulliver goes to Japan by sea after receiving a letter of recommendation from the King of Luggnag to the Emperor of Japan.
8. In Japan, Gulliver is taken to the Emperor.
9. In Japan, Gulliver asks not to have to trample on the crucifix. The Dutch traders, the only Europeans normally allowed in Japan, are required to do so.
10. Gulliver goes by sea to the Netherlands, on a Dutch vessel sailing from Japan. Then he sails from Amsterdam to England.

Suggested Essay Topics

1. Discuss the way reality differs from Gulliver's native expectations in the case of the Struldbruggs.
2. Discuss the Struldbruggs as still another example of Swift's emphasis on human frailty.
3. Discuss the role of religion in these chapters.
4. Discuss Japan as the only real non-European country described to any extent in *Gulliver's Travels.*

SECTION FIVE

Part IV: A Voyage to the Country of the Houyhnhms

Chapters 1 and 2

New Characters:

James Welch: *Mutineer on the* Adventure, *who sets Gulliver ashore on an island*

The Yahoos: *animal-like, savage human beings in the country of the Houyhnhms*

The Dapple-Gray: *Houyhnhm (rational horse) who protects Gulliver and asks him about his country*

The Sorrel: *servant of the Dapple Gray*

Summary

Gulliver spends about five months at home in England. With his wife pregnant, he accepts the captaincy of the *Adventure,* a merchant ship. New sailors to replace those who die of disease are taken on at Barbados. They turn out to be pirates and mutiny against Gulliver, who is held prisoner by them. James Welch, a mutineer, tells Gulliver that the decision has been made to set Gulliver ashore at the first landing-place. Gulliver lands on a strange island, where he is attacked by ugly, disgusting, animals. He is rescued by a horse, who is greeted by another horse; they seem to be conferring together like humans. They examine Gulliver, amazed at his clothing. Gulliver speaks to the horses and is amazed to discover that they neigh in a language. Gulliver gradually learns their language. He hears the word "Yahoo," and learns it.

In Chapter Two, Gulliver finds horses living in a crude sort of building. He discovers that the Yahoos are in fact human beings, although of a filthy and disgusting nature. They are forced to serve the horses, who are called Houyhnhms; they pull a sort of sledge carrying a Houyhnhm. Gulliver refuses to eat the raw flesh that the Yahoos eat; he drinks cow's milk and eventually makes a kind of cake from oats (oats are the Houyhnhms' food). To Gulliver's amazement, the horses are more civilized and more humanlike, except in form, than the Yahoos.

Analysis

Gulliver's treatment at the beginning of each voyage gets worse; on his fourth voyage, he becomes a captain but his own men turn against him. The Yahoos are at first described as strange animals and are only gradually revealed to be humanlike. Here, Swift gives the reader role-reversal; the horses are rational and intelligent and the humans are the disgusting beasts. At first, the Houyhnhms do not realize that Gulliver is a Yahoo because of his clothes; eventually, they see him naked. The Houyhnhms treat Gulliver well and with civility, while the Yahoos treat him disgustingly. In many philosophical works, horses had been treated as examples of non-intelligent beings; Swift is cleverly reversing this idea. What some people have called Swift's misanthropy comes out: the disgusting Yahoos are really humans. In the modern world, the word "Yahoo" is often used to mean someone who is extremely boorish.

Study Questions

1. In what capacity does Gulliver go on his fourth voyage?
2. How does he get to the land of the Houyhnhms?
3. Who does he first meet there?

4. What are the Yahoos?
5. What are the Houyhnhms?
6. What amazes Gulliver in this country?
7. What do the Houyhnhms think of Gulliver at first?
8. How do they treat him?
9. What does Gulliver do about food in the land of the Houyhnhms?
10. What is the attitude of the Yahoos to Gulliver in these chapters?

Answers

1. On his fourth voyage, Gulliver is the captain of a ship.
2. Gulliver's crew mutinies and puts him ashore at the first land they reach.
3. At first, Gulliver meets disgusting, repulsive animals.
4. The Yahoos are extremely degraded, animal-like human beings. They are the first forms of animal life Gulliver sees in the land of the Houyhnhms. Some of them serve the Houyhnhms.
5. The Houyhnhms are intelligent, rational, horses, and they are the most advanced form of life in their country.
6. Gulliver is amazed that horses are able to communicate in a language that Gulliver can learn. They live in buildings, and are generally intelligent.
7. The Houyhnhms at first think Gulliver is not exactly the same form of life as the Yahoos, because of his clothing.
8. The Houyhnhms treat Gulliver well and hospitably.
9. Gulliver is unable to eat the oats the Houyhnhms eat. Finding the Yahoos' food disgusting, he drinks milk and makes cakes of oats.
10. The Yahoos attack Gulliver; he has to be rescued by two Houyhnhms.

Suggested Essay Topics

1. Discuss role-reversal between species in these chapters.
2. How human are the Yahoos in these chapters, and how are they presented by Swift? Discuss.
3. Discuss human imperfection and degradation as depicted in the contrast between the Houyhnhms and the Yahoos in these chapters.
4. Discuss Gulliver's attitude toward Houyhnhms and Yahoos in these chapters.

Chapters 3, 4, and 5

Summary

Gulliver learns the language of the Houyhnhms. His master is amazed at his ability, so uncharacteristic of the Yahoos, and is curious about Gulliver's origin. Gulliver explains his origin, having difficulties because certain human concepts can be explained only with great difficulty in the Houyhnhms' language. Gulliver has to say "the thing which is not" because there is no word for "lie" or "falsehood." When Gulliver is accidentally seen naked, the Houyhnhms realize that he is of the same species as the Yahoos, but differs only in walking on the two hind feet. The Houyhnhms have great difficulty in believing that Gulliver comes from a country in which human beings are rational beings.

In Chapter Four, Gulliver learns that the Houyhnhms believe that the purpose of language is to communicate facts. To "say the thing which is not" defeats the purpose of language. They have difficulty believing that in Gulliver's country people ride horses, and they want to know why the horses don't throw and trample their would-be riders. Gulliver explains how horses are bred, and that some of them are castrated. The Houyhnhms think that Gulliver's body is less serviceable than a horse's. Lacking heavy hair all over his body, he is forced to take the trouble of making and wearing clothes. Gulliver tells a story, emphasizing human vices; the Houyhnhms are unable to understand the purpose of

practicing these vices, nor can they understand the concepts of power, law, government, war, or punishment.

In Chapter Five, Gulliver discusses the causes of war and religious disputes, and has great difficulty making the Houyhnhms understand. The idea that a soldier, whose job is to kill people, could be held in great regard is also very difficult for them to understand. When weapons are explained, the Houyhnhm to whom Gulliver is speaking (the dapple-gray) says that humans in Gulliver's country possess not reason, but some quality to increase their vice. Gulliver describes lawyers as people whose profession is to try to prove that black is white, and *vice versa.* He describes judges as being subject to bribes, and says they don't decide cases according to their merits. Lawyers, Gulliver concludes, are totally unlearned and ignorant outside their trades.

Analysis

In these chapters, Swift has Gulliver describe aspects of human life in the most negative, cynical, terms imaginable. The possibility of judges being honest is denied. Religious differences are trivialized; the idea of lawyers being learned outside their own discipline is denied. Swift, and Gulliver, are in fact giving a highly distorted account of European life, contrasting with the simple, Utopian life of the Houyhnhms.

The influences of Thomas More's *Utopia* and Plato's *Republic* are evident in this section. The real world is deliberately depicted as worse than it is to make the ideal society, here that of the Houyhnhms, look so much better. The bitterness of the aging Swift has also been put forward by scholars as a reason for putting harsh words in Gulliver's mouth. What we have is an intensification of the explanation of Gulliver's country to the King of the Brobdingnagians. There, Gulliver was explaining his country, and the King was shocked by the existence of firearms. Gulliver, having learned from that journey, now describes his country in less positive terms. However, the Houyhnhms are unable to understand even the existence of war. The Brobdingnagians are practical rather than theoretical, in what Swift thinks is a healthy manner. The Laputans are theoretically oriented to a ridiculous extent. The Houyhnhms live a simple, rustic, uncorrupted existence, as portrayed in *Utopia,* Plato's *Republic,* or

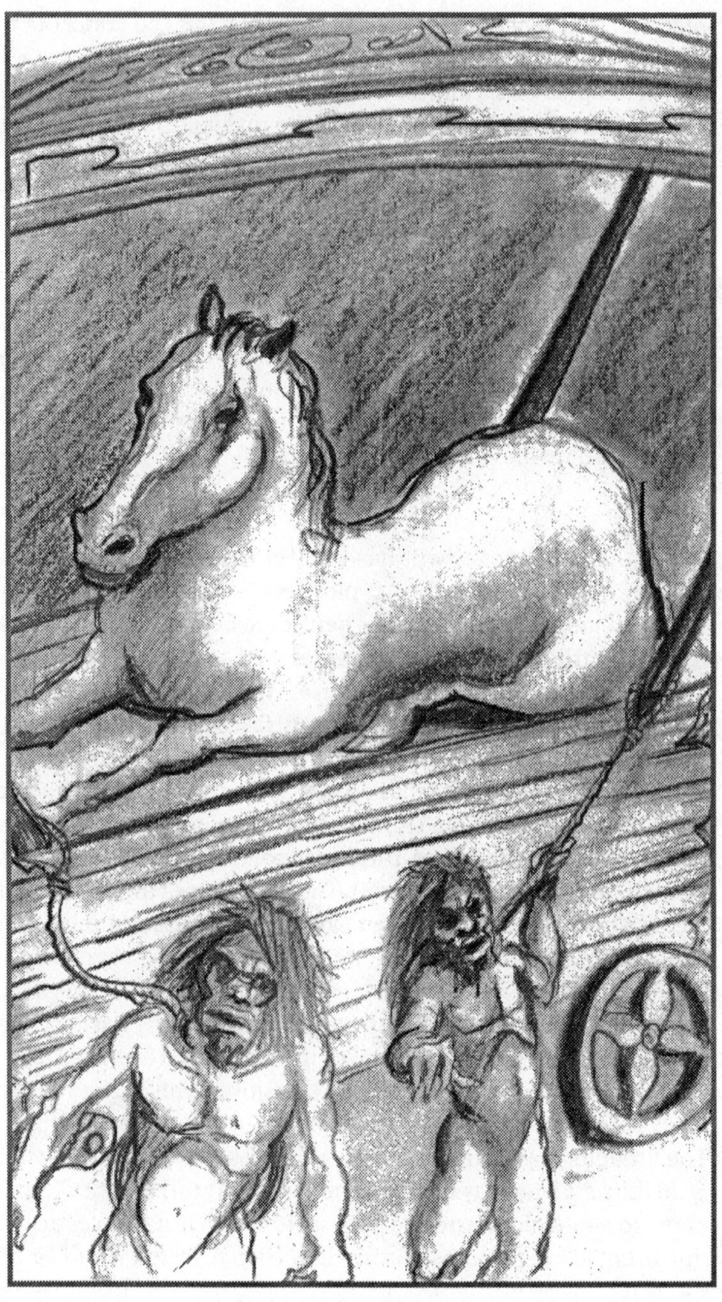

even the Garden of Eden. Are they the true heroes of *Gulliver's Travels*? They are certainly Gulliver's heroes, but are they Swift's? George Orwell wrote that when he read *Gulliver's Travels* as a child, he was so literal-minded as to think so. The reader gets only a hint of Swift's attitude in these chapters.

When the Houyhnhms say that communication is the only purpose of speech, the reader is reminded of the unsympathetic professor in the Academy of Lagado. Having a similar conception of language, he wants to eliminate speech by having people carry symbols of the things they might talk about instead of speaking of them. In both cases, reason is being pushed too far. As will be seen in later chapters, the Houyhnhms are creatures of pure reason who lack sentiment, at least in some respects. They are inhuman in feeling, which is not surprising because they are not humans but horses. A modern science-fiction writer might substitute robots. Swift, as a clergyman, did not believe in the idea, beginning to develop in his time, that pure reason could solve all problems.

Study Questions

1. What is the significance of the phrase "the thing which is not" in these chapters?
2. What do the Houyhnhms discover about Gulliver's physical appearance?
3. What are they unable to understand about a country where horses serve humans?
4. What political concepts are the Houyhnhms unable to understand?
5. How does Gulliver characterize religious disputes in speaking to the Houyhnhms?
6. How does he characterize soldiers?
7. How does he characterize lawyers?
8. How does he characterize judges?
9. Why, according to Gulliver, are learned lawyers not teachers?
10. What does the dapple-gray think when Gulliver explains weapons?

Answers

1. "The thing which is not" is the way Gulliver characterizes a lie or falsehood, a concept unknown to the Houyhnhms.
2. When Gulliver is accidentally seen naked, the Houyhnhms discover that he differs in few major respects from a Yahoo. They had previously been misled by his clothes.
3. They are unable to understand why horses, being larger and stronger, can be compelled to serve humans.
4. The Houyhnhms are unable to understand the concepts of power, war, law, government, or punishment.
5. Gulliver, in speaking to the Houyhnhms, characterizes religious disputes as trivial.
6. Gulliver characterizes soldiers as people who are highly esteemed for their ability to kill people.
7. Gulliver characterizes lawyers as men whose profession is to try to prove that black is white and *vice versa.*
8. Gulliver characterizes judges as being subject to bribes and never deciding cases according to the merits.
9. According to Gulliver, lawyers are totally ignorant outside their own field.
10. When Gulliver explains weapons, the dapple-gray says that humans in Gulliver's country possess not reason, but some quality to increase their vice.

Suggested Essay Topics

1. Discuss the Houyhnhms as totally reasonable creatures who lack words to describe certain concepts.
2. Are the Houyhnhms believable? Discuss.
3. Discuss how Gulliver describes human imperfection and frailties in these chapters.
4. Discuss the attitude of the Houyhnhms to human society as described by Gulliver.

Chapters 6, 7, and 8

Summary

Gulliver continues to describe English society to the dapple-gray, and continues to have difficulty explaining human concepts such as money. The Houyhnhm is amazed at human inequality, and at the use by humans of luxuries such as wines and liquors, some of which have to be imported. Gulliver then explains that the bad habits of human beings cause illness, which in turn requires the services of physicians and pharmacists, who often cause rather than prevent death, making them "of special use to husbands and wives who are grown weary of their mates, to eldest sons, to great ministers of state, and often to princes." Gulliver explains that a minister of state is a creature totally exempt from any human emotion except for a violent desire for wealth, power and titles, and who never tells the truth without meaning that it should be thought a lie and *vice versa.* People rise to high office, according to Gulliver, only by undue influence or hypocrisy. The three principal instruments of statecraft are insolence, lying, and bribery. Politicians are, in the last resort, governed by a "decayed wench or favorite footman."

When Gulliver mentions nobility, the dapple-gray notes that among the Houyhnhms, those of certain colors are better-shaped and more intelligent than others, who continue in the condition of servants. The dapple-gray expressed the opinion that Gulliver must be a noble of his own nation. Gulliver denies that he is a noble and says that in England young noblemen are bred from their childhood in idleness and luxury. A weak, deformed body and the like are signs of noblemen, and these noblemen form one body whose consent is needed to pass laws (the House of Lords is referred to).

In Chapter Seven, Gulliver explains how he could so freely describe mankind to a race already too apt to have the worst idea of humans, on account of the Yahoos. He explains that his admiration for the Yahoos had enlarged his understanding, diminishing his opinion of mankind. His master (the dapple-gray) had observed faults previously not noticed. Gulliver admired the Houyhnhms so much that he wanted never to leave them and return to human kind. He has a hard time thinking about leaving a society characterized by every virtue, with no incitement to practice vice. Gulliver states that he extenuated human faults as much as he could while speaking to the Houyhnhms.

After Gulliver finishes his account of his country, his master (the dapple-gray) states that the humans described by Gulliver somehow (he could not conjecture the reason) developed some small pittance of reason, which they use only to increase their natural corruptions and acquire new ones. In return for this, they had lost the physical abilities that the Yahoos still had, such as strength and agility. Owing to humans' gross defect in reason, they lack virtue. Reason is enough to govern a rational creature. The dapple-gray continues that the Yahoos hate one another because of their ugliness, which they can see in others but not themselves. The Yahoos are selfish and unable to share. They fight over food, and sometimes they fight without visible cause, similar to what Gulliver calls a civil war. The Yahoos esteem shining things of a certain color, fight over them, and hide them, being sad when they are unable to find them. He is unable to discover the reason but thinks it similar to human avarice as described by Gulliver. The dapple-gray also describes how the reactions of the Yahoos to a certain rare root are similar to Gulliver's description of human reactions to liquor.

The Yahoos, the dapple-gray continues, are the only animals in his country subject to illness, which is cured by forcing a mixture of their own dung and urine down their throats. Gulliver adds that he has done this himself and successfully cured illness.

According to the dapple-gray, the most deformed Yahoo was the leader. Other Yahoos licked its posterior. They fight over the females of the species. They have a strange disposition to nastiness and dirt. They sometimes pretend to be ill, hard work being the only cure. From the dapple-gray's description, Gulliver also observes that the rudiments of lewdness, coquetry, censure, and scandal exist among the Yahoos.

In Chapter Eight, Gulliver observes the Yahoos, who are very nimble from infancy but very smelly. They are the most unteachable of all animals, but this defect arises from a perverse disposition. They are cunning, malicious, treacherous, and revengeful.

"They are strong and hardy, but of a cowardly spirit." "The red-haired of both sexes are more libidinous and mischievous than the rest." Some Yahoos are kept in huts near the houses of the Houyhnhms, but others are sent to the fields, where they hunt and live in holes in the ground. On one occasion, when Gulliver was bathing, he was attacked and embraced by a female Yahoo inflamed by desire. She gave Gulliver the worst fright of his life. Gulliver roars as loud as he can, and is saved by the sorrel nag.

Gulliver then describes the customs of the Houyhnhms. They have no concept of evil, and believe primarily in cultivating reason and being wholly governed by it. To them, reason teaches them to affirm or deny something only when they are certain. There are no controversies or disputes among the Houyhnhms. The Houyhnhms have no use for systems of philosophy as described by Gulliver, which to them are merely conjecture. Friendship and benevolence are universal among the Houyhnhms; they have decency and civility but no ceremony. They have no excessive admiration of their own colts or foals, but bring them up strictly according to reason. They cease sexual activity after producing one of each sex. Marriages are planned rationally by parents; children are brought up strictly, emphasizing moderation, hard work, exercise, and cleanliness. They have council every four years.

Analysis

The negative characterization of humankind by Gulliver continues. Swift uses dramatic irony to humorous effect when saying Gulliver is placing the best possible construction on things, which are in fact portrayed in the most negative, cynical manner. To a great extent, Swift seems to be satirizing moralists and preachers. Gulliver's admiration of the Houyhnhms and hatred of humankind are clearly seen as excessive; the dapple-gray's description of the Yahoos is an even more excessive, and even absurd, description of mankind. The Yahoos have an irrational attachment to certain shining things, which is clearly comparable to human avarice for gold. To humans, gold is used as a medium of exchange, but it has no apparent use to the Yahoos. The description of illness and cures among the Yahoos is also clearly satirical. It is reminiscent of passages in Plato's *Republic*, to the effect that illnesses and the need for doctors result from our artificial civilization, insufficient exercise, rich food, and other consequences of it. The reader is also reminded of Laputa and Balnibarbi, where artificiality and excessive abstraction have caused neglect of man's natural needs and created poverty. The "noble savages," uncorrupted and living the simple life, are not the Yahoos. The Yahoos have natural physical strength and agility, which has decayed among civilized people. They also have many of the vices of civilization in a less developed form (the libidinous and mischievous red-haired Yahoos presumably represent the Irish).

The Houyhnhms, who are like the Spartans or the citizens of Plato's *Republic,* live a simple, healthy, life totally ruled by reason. However, their family life, which is totally rational, is inhuman because it is lacking in sentiment. Arguably, the Houyhnhms are, like the Laputans, a satire of rationalism and such works as More's *Utopia.* The naive and proud Gulliver sees them as being perfect, like such literal-minded readers as the young George Orwell, who realized when he got older that the Houyhnhms are not the heroes of the book. Their society is potentially totalitarian, as is their idea that total reason means total unanimity. Historically, fictional utopias have been condemned as totalitarian.

The Houyhnhms are not human, and thus lack human passions, which Swift, as a clergyman and Tory, realized. Their form of society, as Gulliver does not realize, may be appropriate for horses but not for humans. In addition, they have no concept of government, but have assemblies at intervals. They have no concept of punishment, but youths who win contests of endurance are praised; therefore, they have the concept of reward. They lack human passions, but are generous and hospitable, even to Gulliver. The careful reader will notice these contradictions, which further undermine the idea that the Houyhnhms are Swift's heroes. Nothing, characteristically, is said about any religious beliefs on their part. Religion is for human beings only (but nothing is said about the Yahoos having any religious belief, either).

Study Questions

1. How does Gulliver characterize doctors in speaking to the dapple-gray?
2. How does he characterize great ministers of state?

3. How does he characterize noblemen?
4. How does Gulliver characterize his own explanations of society in his own country in these chapters?
5. What is the main defect of humans as described by Gulliver, according to the dapple-gray?
6. Why do the Yahoos hate one another?
7. Why are they the most unteachable of all animals?
8. What is the main belief of the Houyhnhms?
9. How is their family life organized?
10. How are they governed?

Answers

1. Gulliver characterizes doctors as needed because of the diseases resulting from the complexity and artificiality of human civilization; they cause death more often than they prevent it.
2. According to Gulliver, great ministers of state are totally exempt from any human emotion except for a violent desire for wealth, power, and titles.
3. Gulliver says that noblemen are bred from childhood in idleness and luxury and thus have weak, deformed, bodies.
4. Gulliver claims to have extenuated human faults as much as he could while addressing the Houyhnhms.
5. The dapple-gray says that the main defect of human beings as described by Gulliver is their lack of reason. As a result, they lack virtue. Reason is enough to govern a rational creature.
6. The Yahoos hate one another because of their ugliness; they are unable to see their own ugliness but are able to see that of other Yahoos.
7. The Yahoos, according to Gulliver, are the most unteachable of all animals due to a perverse disposition. They are cunning, malicious, treacherous, and vengeful.

8. The main belief of the Houyhnhms is cultivating reason and being wholly governed by it.
9. The family life of the Houyhnhms is organized according to reason, with mating and childbirth planned entirely according to reason. Children are brought up strictly.
10. The Houyhnhms are governed by a council meeting every four years.

Suggested Essay Topics

1. Discuss Gulliver's attitudes toward the Houyhnhms, the Yahoos, and the English. How do these attitudes relate to one another?
2. Compare and contrast Gulliver's attitude toward the Houyhnhms with that of Swift, as expressed in these chapters.
2. Discuss irony in these chapters.
3. Discuss the attitude of the dapple-gray to Gulliver and his country (as described by him) in these chapters.

Chapters 9 and 10

New Character:

Member of Assembly of Houyhnhms: *proposes to eliminate the Yahoos*

Summary

The Houyhnhms hold a grand assembly about three months before Gulliver's departure; the dapple-gray is a representative. The members debate (the only debate they ever held) whether to eliminate the Yahoos. The Yahoos had not always been in the country of the Houyhnhms; two appeared together on a mountain long ago, produced by mud or by the sea, and proceeded to multiply. To control them, the Houyhnhms killed some and tamed the rest. Asses would make better domestic animals. The dapple mentions Gulliver, and suggests that the first Yahoos to arrive in the land of the Houyhnhms came by sea like Gulliver and gradually degenerated and became more savage. The Yahoos should be eliminated by castration, just as Gulliver's people castrate Houyhnhms.

Gulliver goes on to say that the Houyhnhms have no writing; all their knowledge is traditional. They have no need for physicians. They know a little astronomy, and they are great poets. They build wooden houses, and they use parts of their hooves the way people use their hands, with great dexterity. They use stone tools and crude vessels of earth and wood. They die only of old age, unless there are accidents, and feel neither joy nor grief at deaths in their families. In one case, a mare arrived very late for an appointment because her husband "retired to his first mother." She was delayed because of the necessity of consulting her servants as to where the body should be placed. Their only concept of evil relates to the Yahoos.

In Chapter 10, Gulliver describes how the dapple-gray makes a room for him outside the house, and how he makes clothes from the skins of animals and Yahoos. Gulliver is glad to be away from human follies. He speaks (only when spoken to) to several guests of his master on occasion. Their conversations are mostly on philosophical matters or ancient traditions. His attitude toward his family, friends, and countrymen becomes more and more negative.

Gulliver's happiness is disrupted when his master tells him that the Assembly has disapproved of a Yahoo being treated almost like a Houyhnhm. Attempts were made to persuade him, since the Houyhnhms have no conception of compulsion, to either treat Gulliver like other Yahoos or expel him from their land. Those Houyhnhms who had seen Gulliver opposed the first alternative, fearing that he might organize the Yahoos to destroy the Houyhnhms' cattle.

Gulliver faints. After he comes to he is allowed two months to build a boat with the help of the dapple-gray's servants. He does so, kisses his master's hoof, and sails off to an island he had seen with his pocket telescope.

Analysis

Swift here puts in the mouth of the dapple the theory that the Yahoos are degenerate humans, who have come from overseas like

Gulliver. Role reversal is again emphasized for satiric and humorous purposes: horses will castrate humans. Totally rational beings merely exhort; there is no need to compel, since totally rational beings must follow reason. This, like other Utopias, is not really a free society; in fact to disobey would be to lose one's character as a reasonable creature.

The Houyhnhms inhumanely do not mourn. Gulliver's servility, actually a continuation of his cooperation on the other voyages, is shown by his desire to remain permanently with the Houyhnhms and his kissing the dapple's hoof. His foolishness is shown by the fact that he faints. The idea that the weak and compliant Gulliver would, if not expelled, lead the Yahoos to destroy the Houyhnhms' cattle is another example of Swift's irony. According to many critics, the Houyhnhms represent the extreme of reason, while the Yahoos are symbolic of the extreme of appetite. According to this theory, Swift thought "the golden mean" between these two extremes, an idea derived from Aristotle, to be desirable. Swift's ideal would be the King of Brobdingnag. Other critics have felt that Swift's bitterness against the whole human race is being reflected. In a famous letter to Alexander Pope, written in 1725, Swift said that human beings are not rational but merely capable of reason. The dapple-gray and his servant are also not depicted as devoid of human feelings. Clearly, however, the Houyhnhms' proposal to exterminate the Yahoos is not admired by Swift, and Gulliver's attitudes are not Swift's. The Houyhnhms are not human and are not the heroes of the book, despite their admirable features.

Study Questions

1. What is the question debated at the grand assembly of the Houyhnhms?
2. What is the proposal made by the dapple-gray at the assembly?
3. What is the Houyhnhms' attitude to death?
4. What does the assembly of the Houyhnhms decide about Gulliver?
5. What is the reason for this decision?

6. What is Gulliver's initial reaction?
7. Why does Gulliver leave the country of the Houyhnhms?
8. What are the circumstances of his departure?
9. What does he do immediately before his departure?
10. Where does he go at first?

Answers

1. At the grand assembly of the Houyhnhms, the question debated is whether to exterminate the Yahoos.
2. The dapple-gray proposes gradual elimination of the Yahoos through castration.
3. The Houyhnhms are neither glad nor sorry when one of them dies. They do not allow a death to distract them from other business for more than a few hours.
4. The assembly of the Houyhnhms decides to either treat Gulliver like other Yahoos or expel him from their land. They are afraid that he might, if treated like other Yahoos, organize them to steal the Houyhnhms' cattle, so they decide on expulsion.
5. The Houyhnhms think that is contrary to reason to treat a Yahoo almost like a Houyhnhm.
6. Gulliver's initial reaction is to faint.
7. Gulliver leaves the country of the Houyhnhms because he has been expelled, the first time this happens in the book.
8. Gulliver is given two months to make a boat, with the help of the dapple-gray's servants.
9. Immediately before his departure, Gulliver kisses the dapple-gray's hoof.
10. Gulliver's first destination is an island he had seen with his pocket-telescope.

Suggested Essay Topics

1. Discuss the Assembly of the Houyhnhms' attitude to the Yahoos and to Gulliver.
2. Discuss the customs of the Houyhnhms, as described by Gulliver in these chapters.
3. Discuss Gulliver's attitude to his enforced departure from the country of the Houyhnhms.
4. Discuss Swift's depiction in these chapters of the Houyhnhms as not being all the same and not entirely dominated by cold, hard reason.

Chapters 11 and 12

New Character:

Captain Pedro de Mendez: takes *Gulliver to Portugal after he is expelled from the land of the Houyhnhms*

Summary

Gulliver sails away from the land of the Houyhnhms in his boat. He hears the sorrel nag, who always loved him, crying out, "Take of yourself, gentle Yahoo." Gulliver plans to go to some uninhabited island with the means to support life and spend the rest of his life alone there, thinking of the virtues of the Houyhnhms. He would rather do this than hold the highest office in the politest court of Europe, so disgusted is he with human beings. He decides to sail to New Holland (Australia). He lands there, but is attacked by naked savages who injure him with an arrow.

He sees a sail in the distance but does not want to go aboard the ship. Several sailors see him and speak to Gulliver in Portuguese, which he understands. They tell him that the captain will take him for free to Portugal. From there, he could return to England. Gulliver is so reluctant to return to England that he has to be tied up and taken by force to the ship.

The captain, Pedro de Mendez, is sympathetic and generous, but Gulliver is so disgusted by human beings that he tries to jump off the ship and swim away. He has to be chained in his cabin. Gulliver briefly describes his experiences to the captain, who begins to believe Gulliver, but the captain compels Gulliver to promise to make no attempts on his life. Gulliver insists, however, that he would rather suffer the worst hardships than live among Yahoos. Gulliver is reluctant to wear clothes that had been worn by another human being. Arriving at Lisbon, he avoids going into the street for some time. When he finally has the courage, he has to put rue or tobacco in his nose to avoid the human smell.

Captain Mendez finally persuades Gulliver to return to England, since it would be impossible to find an island to live alone on. At home, he could be a recluse. An English ship takes Gulliver to his native land. Arriving at home, he feels hatred, disgust, and contempt at seeing his own family, and feels even worse at having been a parent. When Gulliver's wife embraces and kisses him, he faints (he refers to her as "that odious animal"). For years, he is unable to endure his family's presence; their very smell is intolerable. Gulliver immediately buys two horses; next to them their groom is his greatest favorite, because of his smell. He converses with his horses at least four hours daily.

In Chapter 12, Gulliver insists that he is truthful and compares favorably with other travel writers, intending only the public good. He quotes from the Roman poet Virgil to the effect that because he has been unfortunate, it does not mean that he tells lies. The speaker of this statement is Sinon, who persuaded the Trojans to admit the wooden horse into the city, thus causing the fall of Troy.

Gulliver goes on to say that he does not write from the viewpoint of any party, writing without passion, prejudice or will toward anyone. He discusses the possibilities of England taking possession of the lands he has discovered and denies that there would be any point in doing so. It would not be worth the bother of conquering Lilliput, and it would be too difficult to conquer the other countries. As for the Houyhnhms, Gulliver wishes they could send representatives to teach human beings a lesson. The Houyhnhms, like the emperor Augustus, kick back from all sides. In addition, colonial expansion is usually accompanied by serious abuses, but of course not when the English do it.

The week before writing the last chapter, Gulliver says that he has finally begun to sit at dinner with his wife, at the opposite end of a long table, but he still keeps his nose stopped up with rue, lavender, or tobacco leaves. Pride is the worst thing about human beings, Gulliver concludes, but the Houyhnhms lack it.

Analysis

For the first time in the book, Gulliver is expelled. He is very reluctant about leaving or going back to England. He is so disgusted with human beings that he at first faints at their touch. Some critics have expressed the opinion that Swift is depicting Gulliver as insane. He insists that the Houyhnhms are all the same, equally perfect, despite the sympathy he receives from the dapple-gray and the sorrel, which differs from the attitudes of other Houyhnhms, such as some of those at the assembly. He similarly thinks that all human beings are equally offensive, despite his generous treatment by Captain Pedro de Mendez, which contrasts starkly with Gulliver's own descriptions of human beings in general. Gulliver's disgust with human beings and his sympathy with horses after his return are ridiculous, and clearly indicate that Gulliver is here not a mouthpiece for Swift's opinions.

Gulliver's statements of his purpose sometimes express irony. After having castigated all mankind repeatedly in the strongest terms, he says he has no passion, prejudice, or ill-will toward anyone (there is similar irony, in this case deliberate, in the writings of the ancient Roman historian Tacitus). The first of the Latin quotations clearly refers to the stratagem of the Trojan horse, and may possibly indicate that Gulliver is being tricked when he thinks that the Houyhnhms are perfect. The other Latin quotation, which implies that anyone going too far in praising the Emperor Augustus will kick back like a horse, has given rise to controversy because Augustus appears in a negative light in Luggnagg. Augustus symbolizes authority and power; Gulliver admires them without qualification, unlike Swift.

The denunciation of colonization, which ironically exempts the English, is closer to Swift's viewpoint. As a Tory, he was against activities that might lead to war. Obviously, the vain and not overly bright Gulliver, who prefers horses to his own family, is not put forward by Swift as a hero to be admired without qualification.

Study Questions

1. What is the last thing a Houyhnhm says to Gulliver when he departs?
2. What does Gulliver plan to do after leaving the land of the Houyhnhms?
3. Who are the first human beings Gulliver meets after leaving the country of the Houyhnhms?
4. Who are the next human beings Gulliver meets?
5. How does Gulliver react to their offer to take him back to Europe?
6. How does Captain Mendez treat Gulliver?
7. What is Gulliver's reaction to his rescue?
8. What happens to Gulliver when he returns to his family?
9. What does Gulliver insist in Chapter 12?
10. What does Gulliver say about colonization?

Answers

1. The sorrel nag says when Gulliver is leaving, "Take care of yourself, gentle Yahoo."
2. Gulliver plans to spend the rest of his life contemplating the virtues of the Houyhnhms alone on an island.
3. The first human beings Gulliver meets after leaving the country of the Houyhnhms are savages who wound him with an arrow.
4. The second group of human beings Gulliver meets are Portuguese sailors, who say that their captain will take him back to Europe for free.
5. Gulliver utterly opposes the idea of returning to Europe; he has to be tied up and taken by force to the ship.

6. Captain Mendez treats Gulliver with great kindness and generosity.
7. Gulliver tries to swim away from the ship and has to be chained in his cabin.
8. Gulliver is embraced and kissed by his wife, but faints in disgust.
9. Gulliver insists on his truthfulness and impartiality.

10. Gulliver opposes colonization as pointless, dangerous and also inhumane, at least as practiced by foreigners.

Suggested Essay Topics

1. In these chapters, Gulliver strongly criticizes pride but displays it himself. Discuss.
2. Discuss dramatic irony in these chapters.
3. Discuss places in the last chapter where Swift is expressing his own opinions.
4. Discuss humor in the last two chapters.

SECTION SIX

Sample Analytical Paper Topics

The following paper topics are designed to test your understanding of the work as a whole and to analyze important themes and literary devices. Following each question is a sample outline to get you started.

Topic #1

Swift was known as an ironist. Show how Swift uses irony in the book to strengthen the points he is making.

Outline:

I. Thesis Statement: *In the book, Swift uses irony to strengthen the points he is making.*

II. The point that politics is corrupt

  A. Statesman as acrobats in Lilliput

  B. The King of Brobdingnag's disgust at Gulliver's description of England

  C. The ghosts in Luggnag

  D. The dapple-gray's disgust at Gulliver's description of England

III. The point that human beings are vain

  A. The jealousy that causes Gulliver's fall in Lilliput

B. The jealousy of the dwarfs in Brobdingnag

C. The vanity of the empty ideas of the scientists in Laputa

D. Gulliver's own vanity in thinking he understands everything about human beings and about reason after living among the Houyhnhms

E. Gulliver's criticisms of colonization in the last chapter

IV. Conclusion: Gulliver uses a variety of occasions and techniques to make his points through the use of irony.

Topic #2

Who is the hero, in the sense of most sympathetic character, in *Gulliver's Travels?* Is it Gulliver, the Houyhnhms, or the King of Brobdingnag?

Outline:

I. Thesis Statement: *There are sympathetic characters in* Gulliver's Travels, *but most have flaws; the King of Brobdingnag has the fewest flaws.*

II. Gulliver has the flaws of naiveté and vanity

A. His naive cooperation in all cases

B. His oversimplified ideas that all humans are equally bad and all Houyhnhms are equally good

1. Humans:

a. Feels little gratitude to Mendez

b. Is disgusted by his own family

2. Houyhnhms:

a. The dapple-gray and the sorrel are more sympathetic to him

b. The council is very unsympathetic; Gulliver does not really realize the differences

C. His excessive eagerness to leave his family and go on more voyages even after they turn out disastrously

III. The Houyhnhms are coldly logical and inhuman
   A. They think themselves flawless and perfect
   B. Their inhuman attitude to the family
   C. Their inhuman attitude to death

IV. The King of Brobdingnag is the most sympathetic character
   A. His interest in and sympathy to Gulliver
   B. His disgust at European institutions and inventions such as firearms
   C. His society is flawed but human, unlike that of the Houyhnhms
   D. However, he does laugh when Gulliver just escapes from mortal danger

V. Conclusion: The King of Brobdingnag is the most sympathetic character in *Gulliver's Travels,* although Gulliver thinks otherwise

Topic #3

Swift is famous for his use of linguistic devices, such as the sound of words and the use of lists, to strengthen the atmosphere of parts of his book and to make points. Write an essay discussing the use of these techniques in *Gulliver's Travels.*

Outline:

I. Thesis Statement: *In the book, Swift uses the sounds of words to strengthen his atmospheric effects and tone. He also uses lists, to make polemical points and to increase the effectiveness of ideas he is expressing.*

II. The sounds of words to establish atmospheric effects
   A. Soft-sounding words, using many vowels, to indicate smallness or abstractedness
      1. Smallness: Lilliput, Blefuscu, Nardac
      2. Delicacy and abstractedness: Laputa, Balnibarbi

a. The Language of Laputa, says Gulliver, sounds like Italian

B. Words using many consonants placed together to indicate largeness

1. Brobdingnag, Glumdalclitch

C. Words sound like the neighing of horses to indicate "rational horses"

1. Houyhnhm, Yahoo

III. The use of lists to establish argumentative points and to increase the effectiveness of Swift's ideas

A. Lists to indicate the clash between cultures

1. The list of Gulliver's belongings made by the Lilliputians

2. The list of Gulliver's duties in the agreement with the Lilliputians providing for his freedom

B. Lists to indicate political corruption and human frailty

1. The list of human customs spoken by the King of Brobdingnag

2. The list of English institutions made by Gulliver to the King of Brobdingnag

3. The list of medicines prescribed to cure politicians in the Academy of Laputa

4. Numerous lists indicating human frailty and political corruption in Gulliver's account of his own society to the Houyhnhms

a. The list of bad habits of sailors

b. The list of military weapons and of acts of war

c. The list of medicines, of a disgusting nature

5. The list of characteristics of the Yahoos

IV. Conclusion: Swift effectively uses sounds and lists to strengthen his atmospheric effects and expressions of ideas.

Topic #4

In *Gulliver's Travels,* Swift satirizes such literary *genres* as the travel book and the Utopian work. These satirical techniques increase the effectiveness of *Gulliver's Travels.*

Outline:

I. Thesis Statement: *The effectiveness of* Gulliver's Travels *is increased, and Swift's points strengthened, through satire of the travel book and the Utopian work.*

II. Satire of the travel book, a popular *genre* in Swift's time

1. The original title (*Travels into Several Remote Nations of the World*)
2. The general structure of the book is that of a travel book: there are four voyages
3. The framework of each voyage: arrival and departure
4. The descriptions of the cities (if any) and customs of each country visited
5. The statement about colonization in the last chapter

III. Satire of the Utopian work (description of an ideal society)

1. Description of the customs of the Lilliputians (but no longer observed)
2. The King of Brobdingnag: good king of a less-than-ideal society
3. Laputa and Lagado: rational societies, but too abstracted from reality, with the Academy of Lagado working on potentially good but impracticable inventions
4. The Houyhnhms: a simple uncorrupted, rational society, as in Plato's *Republic,* but inhuman and lacking (mostly) in feeling

IV. Conclusion: The structure of Swift's book is that of a travel book, strengthening Swift's satiric points, many of which appear as travelers' tales. Satire of ideal societies to describe less-than-ideal societies strengthens Swift's ironic emphasis on human imperfection and frailty.

SECTION SEVEN

Bibliography

Swift, Jonathan. *Gulliver's Travels.* Edited by Peter Dixon and John Chalker; with introduction by Michael Foot. Baltimore: Penguin Books, 1967

Erskine-Hill, Howard. *Swift, Gulliver's Travels.* (Landmarks of World Literature) Cambridge: Cambridge University Press, 1993

Probyn, Clive T. *Jonathan Swift, Gulliver's Travels.* (Penguin Critical Series) London: Penguin Books, 1989

Tippett, Brian. *Gulliver's Travels* (The Critics Debate). Atlantic Highlands, N.J. Humanities Press International, 1989

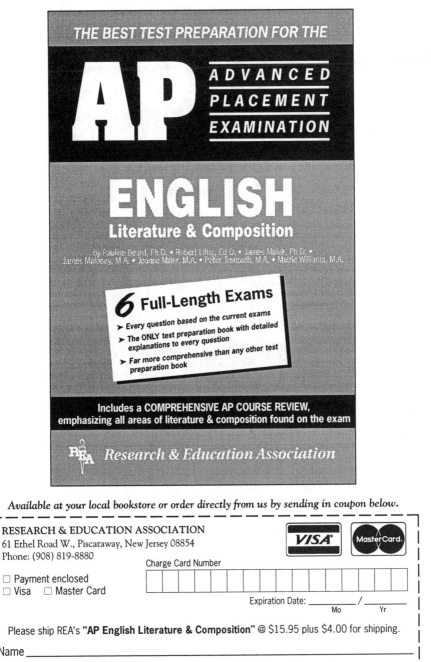

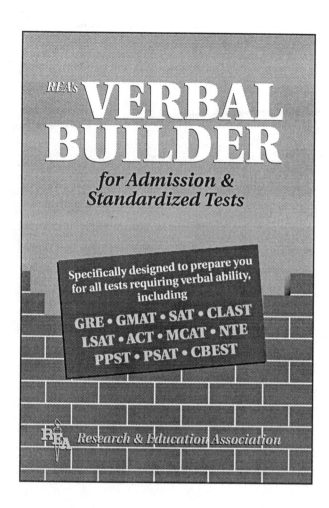

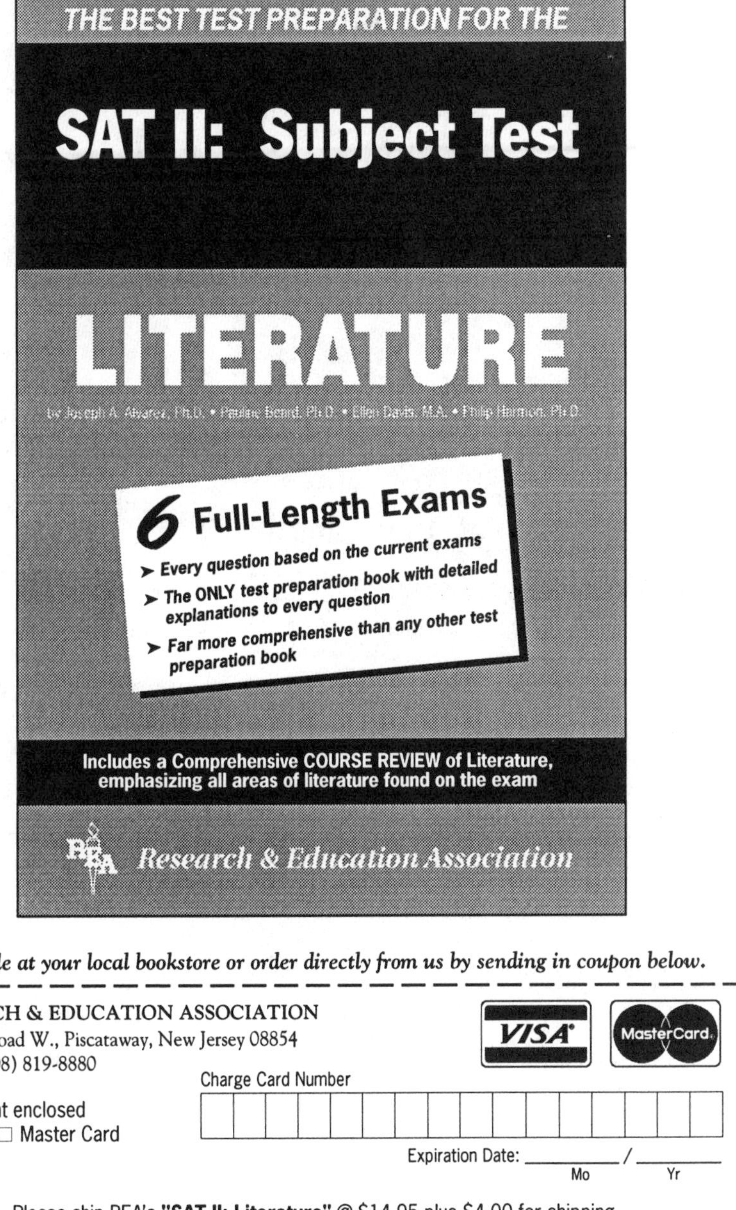

THE BEST TEST PREPARATION FOR THE
SAT II: Subject Test
LITERATURE
by Joseph A. Alvarez, Ph.D. • Pauline Beard, Ph.D. • Ellen Davis, M.A. • Philip Harmon, Ph.D.
6 Full-Length Exams
➤ Every question based on the current exams
➤ The ONLY test preparation book with detailed explanations to every question
➤ Far more comprehensive than any other test preparation book
Includes a Comprehensive COURSE REVIEW of Literature, emphasizing all areas of literature found on the exam
REA Research & Education Association